• educators as audience — how might
it look if it was speaking to
those w/ assumptions or side
by side argument

○Idea of Nation at Risk
reform

Reclaiming the Teaching Profession

"rest of the world is not
waiting for us"

Reclaiming the Teaching Profession

Transforming the Dialogue on Public Education

J. Amos Hatch

ROWMAN & LITTLEFIELD
Lanham • Boulder • New York • London

Published by Rowman & Littlefield
A wholly owned subsidiary of The Rowman & Littlefield Publishing Group, Inc.
4501 Forbes Boulevard, Suite 200, Lanham, Maryland 20706
www.rowman.com

Unit A, Whitacre Mews, 26-34 Stannary Street, London SE11 4AB

British Library Cataloguing in Publication Information Available

Library of Congress Cataloging-in-Publication Data Available

ISBN 978-1-4758-1030-1 (cloth : alk. paper)
ISBN 978-1-4758-1031-8 (pbk : alk. paper)
ISBN 978-1-4758-1032-5 (electronic)

∞™ The paper used in this publication meets the minimum requirements of American National Standard for Information Sciences Permanence of Paper for Printed Library Materials, ANSI/NISO Z39.48-1992.

Printed in the United States of America

For Mary Ann Hatch and Erin Hatch.

Table of Contents

Preface

We're Not Paranoid: They Are Out to Get Teachers

For years, I apologized for feeling paranoid about the barrage of attacks on my profession. I used to start discussions about educational reform initiatives with statements like, "I'm not a conspiracy theorist" or "I don't want to sound neurotic." However, as time passed and the evidence became so clear, I have stopped being sheepish about my concern that powerful forces are at work to take the public out of public education in the United States.

I am not afraid to name the ways current reform agendas distort the democratic ideals that have defined what education in this country is supposed to be all about. As a teacher, teacher educator, and husband and father-in-law of teachers, I have felt the sting as professionals who have devoted their lives to educating children have been devalued, debased, and demonized by politicians, business interests, and the media. I want to speak up and help give others the words and conviction to speak up about what is being done to hurt schools, teachers, and children in this country.

The first goal of this book is to give my fellow educators (especially teachers and future teachers) a clear overview of the massive effort to dismantle public education, which includes a direct attack on teachers. I detail, and provide a critique of, the shaky assumptions at the foundation of radical education reform. I expose the motives and methods of those who are behind the reform movement and provide counternarratives that educators can use to talk back to those who would destroy our profession and public education. I conclude with strategies we can use to reclaim our professional status and reshape the education landscape.

The task of challenging what has become taken for granted about education in the United States seems daunting, but I take heart from the words of

Erich Fromm: "The fact that millions of people take part in a delusion doesn't make it sane." What is happening to public schools and public school teachers is crazy. But our enemies are not the millions of ordinary men and women who have become deluded by the distorted images of teachers and schools generated by the propaganda of media-savvy reformers.

Our enemies are the powerful philanthropists, politicians, business moguls, and education entrepreneurs who create the distortions and finance the propaganda. As educators, we need to talk back to power by exposing the truth about education reform and offering sane, professional alternatives to the market-based makeover of public education promoted by our antagonists.

I try to write as if the reader and I were colleagues talking over coffee. I rely on plain language and solid support to make the case that our profession is being hijacked by powerful individuals who are more interested in having their own way than improving the life chances of children in America. I offer examples that have worked for others and suggestions for action from those who have successfully fought for teachers and schools.

I include footnotes throughout to take interested readers to more detail about the assertions I am making, to provide warrant for my arguments, and to offer sources of support for the case I hope my fellow educators will make. I try to provide insight, evidence, and inspiration that I hope will embolden my colleagues as we fight to protect our schools, our profession, and our democratic society.

The book is organized into two parts. In "Part I: Debunking the Assumptions of the Education Reform Agenda," I describe the depth and breadth of efforts to dismantle public schooling in the United States. Treating each assumption as its own chapter, I lay out ten assumptions upon which current educational reform efforts are based:

1. Public schools are failing.
2. Teachers are inept.
3. Teachers will only work hard to avoid punishment or earn external rewards.
4. Standards-based testing for accountability is the best way to reform schools.
5. Test scores accurately assess what teachers are teaching and students are learning in school.
6. Public schools need to be privatized.
7. Business models have direct application to education.
8. Teachers' unions are a major reason why schools are so bad.
9. Alternative teacher licensure programs are better than traditional teacher education.
10. Wealthy individuals, entrepreneurs, and politicians know more about education than school professionals.

Across the ten chapters in Part I, I systematically debunk each of the assumptions, making clear the half-truths and outright misrepresentations on which the case for reform rests. In each chapter, I present talking points that directly challenge the defective, disingenuous, and duplicitous logic behind reformers' assumptions. The aim is to give teachers, other educators, and our allies tools for talking back to radical education reformers.

"Part II: Speaking Truth to Power" builds on the case made in Part I by exposing the "powers that be" behind radical educational reform and providing alternative narratives, examples of effective resistance, and strategies for countering the efforts of those out to dramatically alter public schooling in the United States. The three chapters in Part II identify the powerful individuals and entities behind the education reform movement and suggest strategies for standing up and speaking truth to power.

"Chapter 11: Exposing the Forces Behind Educational Reform" unmasks the forces and motives that are driving contemporary educational reform, spelling out who the movers and shakers are, how their money and influence are used to shape education policy and practice, and how they are interconnected with others who have similar aims. The goal is to expose the complex and powerful network of forces aligned to demean our profession and reconfigure education in America.

In the concluding chapters of Part II, I offer educators an alternative to being defined as inferior by outside forces. In "Chapter 12: Talking Back to Those Who Would Destroy Public Education," I provide stories of teaching that directly counter the master narrative of school failure and teacher ineptness that dominates discussions of education today. The chapter gives teachers words for articulating educational purposes that are forgotten, ignored, or devalued in the scripted discourse of education reform.

Subsections for chapter 12 are organized around a set of meaningful purposes for public education:

1. to prepare students for full democratic participation;
2. to maximize every student's human potential;
3. to prepare students to be active learners for life; and
4. to prepare students to improve the world they will inherit.

Each purpose elevates the professional role of teachers and relies on rich curriculum, excellent instruction, and informed assessment. Articulating these purposes provides a way for professional educators to "guard the meaning" that is being washed away by the market-driven, test-obsessed agenda of contemporary reform.

The concluding chapter includes specific strategies that experienced, new, and future educators can use to keep their work meaningful and to do what must be done to protect public education, preserve our profession, and provide quality schooling for the generations of students to come. Headings for subsections in "Chapter 13: Strategies for Reclaiming Our Profession" include:

1. Talk Back to the Forces Out to Destroy the Teaching Profession
2. Don't Participate in Your Own Degradation
3. Speak Up About What's Best for Children
4. Speak Up About What's Best for Our Society
5. Engage in Union Activities That Protect the Profession
6. Join with Others to Influence Public Opinion and Education Policy Making
7. Take the High Ground, Guard the Meaning, Redefine High-Quality Education.

This concluding chapter includes examples of how the suggested strategies have been enacted by individuals and groups who are fighting for public education and the teaching profession. Also provided are references to specific resources (e.g., websites, organizations, blogs, texts, and other media) that support teachers' efforts to reclaim our professional status, while defending American education from those who want to privatize it.

It's not paranoia if they are indeed out to get us. My goal is to make the very real threats to public education visible so that they can be recognized, understood, and effectively countered. I want teachers at all levels to be reminded of the importance of our work, to see that we don't have to let others define us as what's wrong with education, and to join with colleagues in reclaiming our professional integrity. As I write this, it seems like the low point in my 30+ years in the field of education. This book is my attempt to help create a brighter future for teachers, schools, our society, and its children.

Acknowledgments

It's hard to make a book. It's impossible to do it alone. To finish this book in good time, I needed to take a professional development leave from my on-campus responsibilities at the University of Tennessee. I am grateful to my department head, Sherry Bell, and my dean, Bob Rider, for supporting my application for that leave. I especially want to thank my coworkers in the Urban-Multicultural Teacher Education Program at the university for covering for me while on the semester-long leave. Chonika Coleman-King, Patty Stringer-Barnes, Linda McClanahan, and Jessica Stone are wonderful colleagues and friends from whom I learn something important every time we work together; I thank them sincerely for their understanding and support. Special thanks to Jessica Stone, who added to her graduate assistant responsibilities to help with the graphics and back matter of the book.

I am grateful to the professionals at Rowman and Littlefield for all their help in bringing this book to publication. Tom Koerner has been attentive and insightful from the very beginnings of this project, and Carlie Wall has guided the production process with grace and intelligence.

I also want to acknowledge the patience and support of my wife, Deb Hatch, who retired from teaching two years ago. That retirement began earlier than planned, due in large part to the impact of the reform initiatives critiqued in this book. Deb was one of the best teachers I've ever known, and it hurts my heart that her love for children and her commitment to providing the best educational experiences possible for them was not enough to keep her in the classroom. I know this is true for too many teachers, and I hope this book helps our profession regain its rightful place so that teachers like Deb will once again be trusted to do their jobs and provide the kind of education our children need and deserve.

Part I

Debunking the Assumptions of the Education Reform Agenda

The power brokers who have a stake in dismantling public education in the United States are out to get teachers and those who support public education. Those influential individuals and the organizations they run (or manipulate) will be described in detail in Part II. For starters, this section reveals for inspection the case that reformers have made for the educational initiatives that dominate thinking about American schooling in the early twenty-first century.

Part I details ten assumptions on which efforts to remake schooling are based and then shows how keeping these assumptions unexamined serves the purposes of those who promote current educational reforms. Each assumption is systematically debunked in an effort to meet the goals of providing some words for talking back to power, supporting teachers and other educators as they give voice to their frustrations, and showing what's at the root of the faulty assumptions on which radical education reform is based.

The nature of assumptions is that they are taken for granted—they are powerful because the possibility of challenging them never comes to mind. But when they are fabricated, exaggerated, or just flat wrong, as the old axiom says, assumptions make an ass of someone. Unhappily, all educators who see public education as an inherently valuable part of the American landscape are being made to look like asses by the assumptions antagonists use to build the case for taking US schooling apart.

Carefully examining these ten assumptions is essential to challenging what is being taken for granted about contemporary teachers, teacher educators, and schools. The treatment of each of the assumptions is organized as a chapter. Each chapter in Part I begins with an overview of the assumption being interrogated. Then that assumption is systematically debunked through the presentation of talking points that directly challenge reformers' faulty or fraudulent assertions. The talking points form the basis for detailed counter-arguments that educators can use to fend off attacks on public education and our profession.

Salient references to traditionally published and Internet-based resources are included in chapter endnotes. These are intended to provide warrant for arguments being made and to give educators and other concerned individuals sources of information they can use to bolster the case against the takeover of public education.

Chapter One

Assumption 1

Public schools are failing

THE ASSUMPTION

Without the assumption that US schools are an abject failure, there is no need for the kind of sweeping reforms that are being foisted on us. Unless they can portray the failure as absolute and comprehensive, they cannot argue for the kind of sea change they have in mind. It would sound lame to say that most public schools in the United States are doing very well, but some are struggling.

They would never point out that schools in affluent and middle-class neighborhoods produce test scores that are as good as or better than national scores for the countries they purport to be superior to our failing American schools. They would never remind their target audience that US public schools take and test all comers, while schools in competing countries serve largely homogeneous populations and test only students who have survived being weeded out in the younger grades. [1]

The powerful forces behind educational reform today have successfully created the overriding impression that schools are terrible. Think tanks and commissions sponsored by wealthy individuals who want to dismantle public education pump out reports based on cherry-picked data that detail the dismal condition of American education. The media sensationalize these reports, selecting the most damaging assertions for their headlines and screen scrolls. Politicians from all over the ideological spectrum pile on, making sure that voters know that they know how bad schools really are.

It's no wonder that the premise that America's schools are failing is unchallenged. The propaganda machine run by those with all the power is

3

very efficient. It has become unthinkable to argue that schools are even okay. Who would dare blur the perfect negative portrayal by pointing out the good and great things about US schooling? Yes, the notion that public schools are failing has reached the status of an assumption. For those in power, that means that extreme measures are justified. Why waste time debating the actual need?

As teachers and others who want to save public education, we need to challenge this assumption as a starting place for resisting the takeover of our schools. We need a counternarrative to the story of absolute failure that is being told by those who are out to get us. Our story does not have to be that schools are all good to counter their story that schools are all bad.

Our story can be about how setting schools up for failure actually serves the purposes of those who want to put public education into private hands.[2] Our story can be real, with nuances and shades of gray. It can stand in contrast to the black-and-white melodrama of absolute failure. Our story can foreground the benefits of public education for all the children in American schools, directly countering the dismal tale that serves the ends of a few. This whole book is about stimulating that counternarrative.

DEBUNKING ASSUMPTION 1

Reformers have manufactured a crisis to achieve their goal of dismantling public schooling. David Berliner and Bruce Biddle used the term "manufactured crisis" to capture the essence of attempts to discredit US education to turn public school control over to market-driven forces.[3] Their work set the precedent for unmasking the tactics and motives of those who stand to gain from the demise of public education in the United States. These authors systematically discredited claims that American schools were indeed failing and revealed the reasons why the manufactured crisis took hold in the consciousness of the American public.

Berliner and Biddle's point continues to be salient today: individuals and organizations that want to privatize public education in the United States have utilized half-truths, doctored data, and propaganda to manufacture an imaginary crisis to achieve their ends. So long as the assumption that a crisis exists and public schools' failure is taken for granted, we will be fighting the battle on the enemy's turf.

We need arguments like those below to advance our position that public schools are not failing. They are not perfect, but their performance has not been nearly as bad as portrayed. Moreover, the story that they are essential to the public good, provide invaluable life experiences to all comers, and have a vital role in preserving democracy is seldom told as the future of American education is discussed.

By many measures, US educational attainment has significantly improved. As reform advocates make their case for drastic restructuring, they forget to mention that high school completion rates have never been higher and the number of Americans attending and completing college has soared over the past several decades.[4]

They decry the lack of rigor in US schooling, but they ignore the fact that college entrance exam scores have returned to levels attained at a time when only privileged college-bound students took the ACT and SAT. The same reform mongers disregard evidence that poor and African American students' scores on these exams have improved dramatically in recent years.[5]

They lament our scores on international assessments, but reformers forget to note that reading and math scores on NAEP tests have never been higher.[6] They point to the low scores of children living in poverty but never acknowledge that disadvantaged American student performance has steadily improved over the past decade in relation to students of the same social class in comparison countries.[7]

We may not be where we would like to be in terms of graduation rates, college attendance, or test scores. But, examples such as these show that it is unfair, misleading, and just plain dishonest for reform advocates to paint with a brush so broad that it covers up the many positive accomplishments of US schooling.

International comparisons used to demonstrate the failure of US schools are based on faulty analyses and unsupported conclusions. It is virtually impossible to draw causal links between international test scores and school quality. Differences between countries' rankings leave out critical factors such as poverty rates, income distribution, immigration rates, social services, who attends school, and who participates in cram courses outside of school.[8]

Still, commissions with a political agenda, think tanks that rely on foundations and powerful corporations for support, and media outlets that search for sensational stories all perpetuate the incessant barrage of school and teacher bashing related to international test score comparisons. To maintain the façade that US schools are total failures, facts like the following are virtually never mentioned.

American students who attend schools where less than 10 percent of students receive free or reduced lunch do as well or better than students anywhere in the world, and US students who go to schools where the poverty rates are less than 25 percent score better than all but four other countries.[9] The United States has the highest poverty rate in the developed world,[10] yet the impact of poverty on test performance is consistently ignored or underweighted as international analyses are completed and conclusions are reported.[11]

For example, researchers recalculated the most recent PISA scores after discovering a sampling error in the US administration of the test that over-represented students from the most disadvantaged schools. Their reanalysis showed that original reports based on flawed data significantly underestimated the performance of American students.[12]

It is clear that poverty and the associated consequences of living in poverty have a profound impact on educational outcomes for children, including their scores on international tests; yet this fact is ignored as reformers generate their arguments for monumental changes in US public schooling.[13] Again, these are only examples of ways that comparison data have been misused to indict American teachers and schools.

Schools that are "failing" in the US receive far fewer resources than schools counted as successful. An important theme in the radical reformers' attack on public schooling is that we are already spending too much on schooling and that "throwing money" at the problems of underperforming schools will not make the problem go away. In fact, other countries with which we are compared pay much higher taxes relative to their GDP to support public education and other civic services[14] at the same time that public spending per pupil is dropping in the Unites States.[15]

Reform advocates argue that adding resources to failing schools has not worked, so why send "good money after bad." In fact, the distribution of resources between have and have-not schools in the United States is stunningly disproportionate. As Linda Darling-Hammond points out,

> International studies continue to confirm that the US education system is also one of the most unequal in terms of inputs. In contrast to European and Asian nations that fund schools centrally and equally, the wealthiest school districts in the US spend nearly 10 times more than the poorest districts, and spending ratios of 3:1 are common within states.[16]

Other nations treat education as a common good that ought to be shared equally among all their citizens. They allocate educational resources in ways that acknowledge that it will cost more to successfully teach the students with the biggest needs.[17] In the United States, where you live and how much your family makes largely determine what kinds of resources your school will have access to. To blame teachers for the poor performance of students who attend poorly resourced schools in poor communities ignores the realities of poverty and their concomitant effects on children's ability to learn.

US public schools take (and test) all comers. Most of the countries with which we are unfavorably compared have largely homogeneous populations, and many have structures built into their education systems that track the most able students into advanced coursework, while moving those less academically competent into alternative tracks or directly into the workforce. That means that the performance of *all* US students, regardless of the diversity of their experiences and capabilities, is being compared with outcomes of a *subset* of international students that is much more narrowly defined.

The accomplishments of American teachers are being ignored or dismissed by powerful forces trying to impose their will on educators. Those forces have effectively created a public discourse that devalues teachers' efforts, misrepresents their motives, and undermines their confidence.

Public schools are not failing. Educators need to make the case that the "crisis" in education is indeed manufactured by those who would destroy public schooling. We need to articulate our accomplishments and expose the loaded methods used to analyze and report international comparison studies. We must find ways to help others see the real value we add to the life chances of the children we teach, especially those who experience the devastating effects of poverty.

NOTES

1. Carnoy, M., and Rothstein, R. (2013, January 28). What do international tests really show about U.S. student performance? Economic Policy Institute, http://www.epi.org/publication/us-student-performance-testing

2. Berliner, D. C., and Biddle, B. J. (1996). *The manufactured crisis: Myths, fraud, and the attack on America's public schools.* Cambridge, MA: Perseus Books.

3. Berliner and Biddle. *The manufactured crisis.*

4. Farhi, P. (2012, March 30). Flunking the test. *American Journalism Review,* http://www.ajr.org/article.asp?id=5280; Sheehy, K. (2013, January 23). Gaps persist despite rising high school graduation rates. *US News,* http://www.usnews.com/education/blogs/high-school-notes/2013/01/23/gaps-persist-despite-rising-high-school-graduation-rates

5. School Leadership Briefing. (2011, May 1). David Berliner: The manufactured crisis revisited, http://www.schoolbriefing.com/1967/the-manufactured-crisis-revisited

6. Banchero, S. (2013, June 27). Primary, middle level students show gains. *The Wall Street Journal,* http://online.wsj.com/article/SB10001424127887323689204578571920489593626.html

7. Carnoy and Rothstein. What do international tests really show about U.S. student performance?

8. Rotberg, I. C. (2014, May 19). Tenuous findings, tenuous policies. *Teachers College Record,* http://www.tcrecord.org

9. Berliner, D. C. (2014). Effects of inequality and poverty vs. teachers and schooling of America's youth. *Teachers College Record, 116*(1), 1–14.

10. United Nations. (2012, April). Progress for children (Report Card 10). UNICEF, http://www.unicef.org/publications/index_62280.html

11. Berliner. Effects of inequality and poverty; Equity and Excellence Commission (2013). *For each and every child: A strategy for education equity and excellence.* US Department of Education, http://www2.ed.gov/about/bdscomm/list/eec/equity-excellence-commission-report.pdf

12. Carnoy and Rothstein. What do international tests really show about U.S. student performance?

13. Carter, P. L., and Welner, K. G. (2013). *Closing the opportunity gap: What America must do to give every child an even chance.* New York: Oxford University Press.

14. Berliner. Effects of inequality and poverty.

15. Banchero, S. (2013). Public spending per student drops. *Wall Street Journal,* http://blogs.wsj.com/economics/2013/05/21/public-spending-per-student-drops

16. Darling-Hammond, L. (2010). *The flat world and education: How America's commitment to equity will determine our future*. New York: Teachers College Press. [p. 120]

17. Levin, B. (2013). Shanghai and Seoul plan higher achievement. *Phi Delta Kappan, 94*(8), 74–75.

Chapter Two

Assumption 2

Teachers are inept

THE ASSUMPTION

Schools are terrible, but it couldn't be because the buildings in lots of communities are falling down around the kids. It couldn't be because lots of kids come to school without having their basic physical, safety, and psychological needs met at home. It couldn't be because schools are being asked to do more and more with less and less. It couldn't be because US schools are trying to serve the needs of all children, including those who have disabilities or don't speak English as their first language. It couldn't be because US citizens invest relatively less on schooling than folks do in the countries with which we compare ourselves.[1]

No, it would muddy the argument to bring in all those complications. The assumption that schools are terrible is explained by the second assumption: teachers are inept. The enemies of public schooling need to maintain the impression that only individuals who are unfit for real professions work in US classrooms.

In the scenario they work hard to create, only the weakest college students select education as a major. Teacher preparation is vapid, and anyone who shows up will be handed a teaching license. New teachers who have other options leave the field once they see how bad the schools are. Those who stay don't know very much and do as little as possible. They take advantage of short workdays and long summers off.

The longer teachers stay in the field, the less they do. Teaching is an easy job that requires little or no specialized training, and teachers do not work hard because they are protected by tenure. In short, everything those who would destroy public education have to say sends the message that teachers are inept.

Teacher bashing has become a national pastime. You can't pick up a newspaper or magazine without reading stories about how bad teachers are. You can't turn on the television or search the Internet without being bombarded with negative portrayals of teachers. Even documentary filmmakers and Hollywood producers are generating movies that show how badly we need to reform our terrible public schools and get rid of our selfish, inept teachers. And you certainly can't sit through a speech from any politician without hearing about how badly we need to clear out the teaching deadwood (and the unions that protect them) so we can reshape our failing schools.

There's a ton of money tied to keeping alive the assumption that teachers are inept. If teachers don't know much and don't work hard, then they need to be given canned programs with scripted lessons. If teachers are not smart enough to develop their own curricula and design their own teaching strategies, then we need publishing companies to produce "teacher-proof" materials to make sure children are being taught. If teachers cannot be relied upon to make sound judgments about student progress, then we need systems of evaluation that make sure kids are learning. Millions upon millions of dollars are spent annually to purchase materials that exist because it is assumed that teachers are inept.[2]

The standards-based accountability movement will be explored in chapter 4, but the point here is that powerful economic and political forces have a vested interest in being sure that teachers are seen as incapable of doing their jobs. Teachers are not up to it, so someone else needs to make decisions about what to teach, how to teach, and how to assess what has been learned. Marketing the materials that are supposed to do what teachers can't do is directly tied to convincing everyone that teachers are inept.

DEBUNKING ASSUMPTION 2

Teachers are easy targets. Teacher morale is at its lowest point in anyone's memory.[3] Education critics portray teachers as those immediately responsible for the failing schools the reformers plan to fix. Teachers are targets of opportunity because they are the faces of education that everyone can relate to. When Americans think of education, the image of a teacher working directly with a set of students is what comes to mind.[4]

Lay citizens don't consider the bigger picture of schooling as a complex endeavor involving elements like governance, finance, infrastructure, politics, taxation, and community. Ordinary Americans don't think in terms of a *system* of education; they focus on teachers in classrooms.[5] The educational reform public relations machine understands this phenomenon and makes teachers the primary target as attacks are orchestrated.

Teachers are portrayed as demons by reformers, politicians, and the media. Even by the arbitrary test-driven standards established by the radical education reformers, the vast majority of teachers are doing a terrific job. However, that part of the story is never told when reports on failing schools are released, politicians make their pronouncements on the dire state of education, and the media package their sound bite–driven coverage.

Reformers have created networks of commissions, think tanks, and lobbyists to crank out misinformation about how bad teachers are. Politicians from both major parties have adopted the rhetoric of the reform agenda and unabashedly, unceasingly blame teachers. Print, broadcast, electronic, and even the entertainment media uncritically transmit the reformers' and their political cronies' message of inept teachers to the public.[6]

One telling example of how this network operates is the 2012 report called "US Education Reform and National Security" prepared for the Council on Foreign Relations by Joel Klein and Condoleezza Rice.[7] The report argues that the poor quality of K-12 schooling in the United States represents a "very grave threat to national security" and calls for more competition and privatization to improve our system. The media broadcast the sensational "finding" that poor teaching is putting our national security at risk. However, they never mention the dissent published at the end of the report, dissent that challenges both the findings of the report and the recommendations.[8]

The demonization of teachers has even become fodder for Hollywood productions like *Waiting for Superman* and *Won't Back Down*, both of which promote privatization schemes by portraying public school teachers as callous, ineffective, and selfish. Teachers are the bad guys in the reform movement's melodrama, and our professional expertise, hard work, and dedication are edited out of the story.

Teachers have been asked to do more with less. Teaching is not just a thankless job given the incessant bashing from all quarters, it is more difficult than ever. New programs, curricula, and teaching approaches are constantly being added at the same time that expectations for improved test scores are escalating. The Common Core State Standards are being rolled out in all but a handful of states, meaning that the materials, lessons, and teaching approaches that teachers have been using (successfully or not) have to be scrapped and new ones developed.

Right behind the core curriculum is a new testing regimen that will put increased pressure on teachers and students. This is only the latest in an endless series of changes that force teachers to adjust to influences outside their control. In spite of reformer public relations campaigns that sell the idea that teaching is so easy anyone can do it, teachers have always had difficult and stressful jobs.[9]

Unlike other professionals who see one client at a time and have space between appointments to prepare and reflect, teachers are engaged 100 percent of the time with large numbers of students, each one having a particular learning style and personality. The simplistic perception that the teacher's role is to stand and deliver instruction masks the complexity of working with young human beings whose physical, social, and psychological needs come with them through the classroom door.

Teachers have never been asked to do more. At the same time, support for teachers and resources for schools have steadily declined. Working conditions for teachers are deteriorating, and teachers' rights to bargain for more support and better working conditions are being stripped away.[10] School buildings in many parts of the country are falling down around students and teachers; students, families, and communities in many places have lost hope; and more and more of children's basic needs are not being met outside the school.[11]

Teachers provide much more than academic instruction. In many communities, they have become the central social unit in the lives of children. Instead of gratitude and respect for the increasing difficulty of teaching, we get more impossible mandates and incessant grief from those who see public education as a place to open up "free markets" and make fortunes.

There is money to be made from teacher bashing. If public school teachers are as bad as we are made out to be, then private enterprise is ready to step in and solve that problem. The assumptions being debunked in this book are the foundation for the ultimate destruction of public education and the eventual privatization of schooling in this country. But making teachers look inept also has major financial payoffs in the short term.

Billions of dollars have been made by testing companies alone because US teachers are so unprofessional and untrustworthy that outside entities are needed to assess whether or not children are learning in school. A 2012 study showed that standardized testing costs the states at least $1.7 billion each year.[12] The whole accountability movement rests on the notion that teachers need to be held to learning objectives that they are unable to create and assess on their own. Even better for education entrepreneurs, more billions can be made producing teacher-proof curricula and test preparation materials because teachers are incapable of getting students ready for the test when left to their own devices.[13]

It's a perfect circle for companies that market "accountability": teachers are incapable of doing their jobs and must be held accountable; we have produced tests to measure the value teachers add each year; we also have produced curricula and test prep materials to ensure that these slovenly teachers know what to teach to improve test scores. The reformers and their entrepreneurial partners create an imaginary need, and then local, state, and federal governments pay massive amounts of money based on the assumption that teachers are inept.

We need a counternarrative that reminds everyone of the intelligence, dedication, and specialized preparation required to be an effective teacher in the challenging circumstances that characterize today's schools. We need to highlight all we do that goes far beyond preparing students to pass tests. We need to let people know that we teach academic content and life lessons that are never assessed on standardized assessments.

We need to tell our story of teaching children what it means to be healthy, successful, and productive human beings. We need to remind the public that we teach all of the students who come through our doors, no matter what their backgrounds or special needs. We need to point out our place as professionals who are vital to the continuation of our nation's democracy, educating the next generation to understand the rights and responsibilities of citizenship.

We need to reclaim our professional status as those who know best what should be learned in school, how it should be taught, and what should be counted as evidence that it has been learned. Further, we should not be afraid to tear away at the elaborate façade educational reformers have created to ensure that teachers are demeaned and public schools are put into private hands.

NOTES

1. Schniedewind, N. (2012). A short history of the ambush of public education. In N. Schniedewind and M. Sapon-Shevin (Eds.), *Educational courage: Resisting the ambush of public education* (pp. 4–22). Boston: Beacon Press.

2. Chingos, M. M. (2012). Strength in numbers: State spending on K-12 assessment systems. Brown Center on Education Policy, http://www.brookings.edu/research/reports/2012/11/29-cost-of-ed-assessment-chingos

3. MetLife Survey of the American Teacher (2013), http://www.metlife.com/teachersurvey

4. Bales, S. N. (2011). Framing education reform: A frameworks message/memo. Frameworks Institute, http://www.frameworksinstitute.org/assets/files/PDF_Education/education_message_memo.pdf

5. Kumashiro, K. K. (2012). *Bad teacher: How blaming teachers distorts the bigger picture.* New York: Teachers College Press.

6. Farhi, P. (2012, March 30). Flunking the test. *American Journalism Review*, http://www.ajr.org/article.asp?id=5280

7. Klein, J. I., and Rice, C. (2012). *US education reform and national security.* Council on Foreign Relations, http://www.cfr.org/united-states/us-education-reform-national-security/p27618

8. Strauss, V. (2012). Best part of 'schools-threaten-national-security' report: The dissents. *Washington Post*, http://www.washingtonpost.com/blogs/answer-sheet/post/best-part-of-schools-threaten-national-security-report-the-dissents/2012/03/20/gIQAe0yaQS_blog.html

9. Hatch, J. A. (1999). What preservice teachers can learn from studies of teachers' work. *Teaching and Teacher Education, 15,* 229–242.

10. Schniedewind. A short history of the ambush of public education.

11. Berliner, D. C. (2014). Effects of inequality and poverty vs. teachers and schooling of America's youth. *Teachers College Record, 116*(1), 1–14; Darling-Hammond, L. (2010). *The flat world and education: How America's commitment to equity will determine our future.* New York: Teachers College Press; Fabricant, M., and Fine, M. (2012). *Charter schools and the corporate makeover of public education: What's at stake?* New York: Teachers College Press.

12. Chingos. Strength in numbers.

13. Ravitch, D. (2010). *The death and life of the great American school system: How testing and choice are undermining education.* New York: Perseus Books.

Chapter Three

Assumption 3

Teachers will only work hard to avoid punishment or earn external rewards

THE ASSUMPTION

The No Child Left Behind Act (NCLB) and the Race to the Top (RttT) initiatives are based on the assumption that teachers are not working hard enough. Again, schools are terrible and teachers are to blame, so how can that be changed? The business leaders and their political cronies who designed NCLB decided that teachers and schools were not doing their job and needed to be held accountable for their failures. There needed to be serious consequences for not making the grade.

An elaborate accountability system based on standardized testing was set up so that schools and teachers who were not producing adequate yearly progress could be identified and punished. The pitfalls of using test scores for assessing children and teachers' performance are taken up in the next chapter. The point here is that an education act backed by both political parties was built on the premise that teachers were not doing their jobs and would only do better with the threat of sanctions to their schools and the potential loss of their livelihoods.

NCLB is emblematic of the well-orchestrated effort to destroy public schools. It was the perfect trap, rigged to appear that the prey were responsible for their own capture. Impossible goals were set, arbitrary standards were established, and when schools did not improve, it was never because of the ridiculous expectations built into the plan.[1] Reformers set educators inside a trap from which there was no escape, and then they pointed at us and

15

said, "See, those inept teachers did not work hard enough to fix our terrible schools, so we need to dismantle public education as we know it."

The Obama administration's Race to the Top approach perpetuates the assumption that teachers are not willing to work hard without some kind of outside motivation. As they rolled out, many of the changes to NCLB looked like an attempt to trade carrots for sticks as tools for motivating schools and teachers. It turned out the sticks were still there, as hundreds of schools have been closed and turned over to private interests; but carrots in the form of large grants to states and districts were used to move the reform agenda along (i.e., adopting the Common Core Standards and using test scores to assess teacher effectiveness).

The idea that educators might be committed individuals with professional and personal integrity who are doing all they can to provide the best education possible for the students they serve is never part of the conversation. Otherwise, what would be the need for carrots or sticks? RttT may have features that appear more favorable than NCLB, but assumptions about teachers are the same: external motivation based on the fear of sanctions or the promise of rewards is necessary to get educators to do their jobs.

DEBUNKING ASSUMPTION 3

NCLB was rigged to ensure that teachers and public schools would be labeled as failures. Even the staunchest advocates for No Child Left Behind legislation have acknowledged that the core strategy of requiring schools to make adequate yearly progress (AYP) or be punished set an impossible task.[2] No one who had actually thought it through believed that 100 percent of the students in American schools could reach "proficiency" by 2014. But as each year unfolded and the percentages of schools not making annual gains that would get them to 100 percent proficiency by 2014 (i.e., AYP) rose exponentially,[3] teachers were blamed for not working hard enough.

Various metaphors have been offered to describe the absurd expectations placed on teachers and schools by NCLB mandates. One analogy likens saying every child will be proficient in reading and math to saying that all US cities will be crime-free by a certain date and, if not, police officers will be disciplined or fired and police departments will be closed or turned over to private companies.[4]

Another metaphor compares NCLB's approach to threatening to punish doctors and hospitals unless 100 percent of American citizens receive adequate health care within a certain time frame.[5] As dumb as these scenarios sound, this was precisely the logic of NCLB: heads would roll unless impossible AYP goals were accomplished.

NCLB policies failed, and teachers were blamed. Fear of being labeled failures and of being fired was supposed to motivate teachers to accomplish the goals of NCLB. Whatever they were doing before their reputations and livelihoods were put in jeopardy was obviously not enough, so teachers needed the threat of sanctions to get them to work harder. As we have seen, NCLB policies were doomed to fail and they did; but did policy makers take responsibility for creating a maze from which there was no escape? No, the victims trapped in the maze were vilified once again.

It is imminently clear that NCLB policies did not work. Independent analyses by the National Research Council[6] and others[7] document the extent of this policy's failure. Teachers were left behind, schools were left behind, and countless children were left behind, especially those in poor communities serving children of color and those whose first language is not English.[8]

Because the original legislation was supported by both parties when it passed in 2001, neither party is in a position to point accusatory fingers across the aisle. No one is taking responsibility for the faulty foundations of NCLB, and no one is willing to tackle rewriting the legislation on which it is based. Instead, the current administration is granting waivers from selected NCLB requirements in exchange for agreements that once again set teachers and public schools up for failure.

Race to the Top initiatives take for granted that threats or rewards are needed to motivate teachers. RttT was created after President Obama's first election victory by Arne Duncan, the newly appointed Secretary of Education. While many teachers and other educators were hopeful that the new administration would abandon the failed education policies of their predecessors, we were soon disappointed. Instead, Secretary Duncan took unprecedented steps to extend the reach of federal involvement in education while maintaining the mind-set that lazy, inept teachers are the problem and that outside factors need to be applied to fuel education reform efforts.

Closely aligned with forces aiming to dismantle public education, the secretary doubled down on the reliance on high-stakes standardized tests to measure reform success. He offered waivers to states willing to capitulate to an array of demands that ultimately undermines the efficacy of public schooling in America.

Some of the most dramatic demands include the following: linking teacher evaluations directly to students' standardized test scores; signing on to implement the Common Core Standards and utilize the associated standardized tests to follow; agreeing to reduce restrictions on the creation of charter schools; expanding alternative routes to teacher licensure; reducing teachers' collective bargaining rights; challenging teacher tenure statutes; and implementing merit pay schemes for teachers and administrators.

The "Race to the Top" label signals an attempt to offer incentives not only to teachers (i.e., merit pay for high test scores), but also to schools, systems, and states for compliance and performance (on the same test scores). It does not matter that these strategies have no support in the literature on school improvement[9] or that they are promoted by private entities that profit from the demonization of teachers and the destruction of public education.

RttT is firmly institutionalized with no end in sight. It remains clear that the federal government is working hand in glove with radical reformers to propagate education policy that depends on the belief that teachers and schools will not do their jobs without the fear of sanctions or the promise of rewards.

Competition is glorified as the driving force behind educational improvement. The current power brokers, inside government and out, believe that competition is inherently good. They are attempting to apply theories of free-market capitalism, which they are sure make American business strong, to strengthen the enterprise of schooling. They think pitting state against state, district against district, school against school, and teacher against teacher in a race for recognition and resources is a winning strategy for US schools.

But, in case carrots don't get the job done, the costs of falling behind in the race (the same old accountability sticks) are ramped up even more under RttT rules. School closing and mass firings are now commonplace in places where reform benchmarks are not being met. It is no surprise, but almost all of these draconian measures are happening in large urban school districts that serve students who are poor, students who are not white, and students who do not speak English as their first language.

It is also no surprise that most of the closed public schools are being replaced by for-profit charters that happen to be at the ready to fill the gap.[10] It turns into a cruel irony that "those needing the most educational resources will get the least, which undermines a fundamental idea of American education—that public education should provide equal educational opportunity for all children."[11]

As teachers, we know that for every winner there are many losers and that it is our professional commitment and expertise that propel meaningful change in schools—not jumping through arbitrary hoops imposed by those who know little or nothing about how learning and teaching happen in real classrooms in real schools. NCLB is the archetype strategy to undermine the credibility to public schools, and it provided a neatly constructed trap that made the teacher prey look like they deserved capture and punishment. RttT has added incentives while keeping the harsh consequences of NCLB; but the incentives require states, districts, and individuals to compete with others who have their own pressing needs.

Neither approach has worked nor will work, and teachers will continue to be blamed for the ineffectiveness of these failed policies. The two elements that bind NCLB to RttT approaches are (a) the assumption that teachers will not work hard unless they are compelled by forces outside their professional integrity and (b) the unquestioned premise that standardized testing for accountability is the centerpiece of educational reform. Teachers must counter the first assumption by pointing out the flaws in believing and applying it, while arguing for our intrinsic commitment to children, learning, and the democratic principles at the core of public education. The wrongheadedness of an overreliance on standardized testing is taken up in the next sections.

NOTES

1. Hess, F. M., and Finn, C. E. (Eds.). (2007). *No remedy left behind: Lessons from a half-decade of NCLB*. Washington, DC: AEI Press.
2. Hess and Finn. *No remedy left behind*.
3. Duncan, A. (2011, March 9). Winning the future with education: Responsibility, reform and results. Testimony given to the US Congress. Washington, DC, http://www.ed.gov/news/speeches/winning-future-education-responsibility-reform-and-results
4. Ravitch, D. (2010). *The death and life of the great American school system: How testing and choice are undermining education*. New York: Perseus Books.
5. Karp, S. (2008). NCLB's selective vision of equalty: Some gaps count more than others. In W. Ayers, G. Ladson-Billings, G. Michie and P. Noguera (Eds.), *City kids, city schools* (pp. 222–223). New York: New Press.
6. National Research Council (2011). *Incentives and test-based accountability in education*. Washington, DC: The National Academies Press.
7. Timar, T. B., and Maxwell-Jolly, J. (Eds.). (2012). *Narrowing the achievement gap: Perspectives and strategies for challenging times*. Cambridge, MA: Harvard Education Press; Ravitch. *The death and life of the great American school system*.
8. Bryant, J. (2013, February 2). The inconvenient truth of education "reform." Campaign for America's Future, http://blog.ourfuture.org/20130202/the-inconvenient-truth-of-education-reform
9. Schniedewind, N. (2012). A short history of the ambush of public education. In N. Schniedewind and M. Sapon-Shevin (Eds.), *Educational courage: Resisting the ambush of public education* (pp. 4–22). Boston: Beacon Press.
10. Bryant. The inconvenient truth of education "reform."
11. Schniedewind. A short history of the ambush of public education. [p. 13]

Chapter Four

Assumption 4

Standards-based testing for accountability is the best way to reform schools

THE ASSUMPTION

To salvage our shipwrecked schools, we need to make inept, lazy teachers toe the line. We have to hold them accountable. Left to their own devices, teachers randomly select what content to cover, when to teach it, and how it will be taught. We need rigorous standards that define exactly what should be taught and when. Left to their own devices, teachers rely on self-serving judgments to decide if students are learning or not. We need tests that generate objective data to assess how well the specific standards are being taught. So goes the logic of standards-based accountability.

The rapid rise of the Common Core Standards is strong evidence for the centrality of this assumption to the reformers' agenda. Adroitly linked to Race to the Top, almost all states have been forced to sign on to these standards to receive federal funding. Never mind that states are historically charged with overseeing the education of their own citizens, reform advocates have found a way to back-door national standards.

At this writing, we have the core standards of a national curriculum in place, and we are witnessing the field-testing of new assessments to measure how well teachers are teaching the new standards. Each state has had its own high-stakes testing regimen in place for years; now the stakes are raised as we double down on a national level.

High-stakes tests are a critical feature of current reform efforts. Outcome measures in the form of standardized test scores are taken to be the driving force for improving school performance. Value-added measures that compare teacher and school performance year to year based on standardized test scores are considered to be the gold standard for measuring educational outcomes.[1]

Critics of public schooling in the United States believe that models from the business world should be used to measure the effectiveness of schools. They are sure that laying down higher expectations for workers and toughening quality control will improve productivity. They have learned from their business experience that quotas must be met or heads will roll. They take test scores to be the products of the educational enterprise, so standards-based accountability makes perfect sense.

Schools give billions of dollars annually to companies that have a vested interest in perpetuating the assumption that standards-based testing is the best way to improve schooling in America. Hundreds of thousands of classroom hours are spent preparing for and taking standardized tests.

The argument that all that money might be better spent on improving school infrastructures or upgrading classroom technology falls on deaf ears. The case that all that classroom time might be better spent on teaching and learning is ignored. When you have all the power, you get to set up your own assumptions. Anyone who challenges the efficacy of standards-based testing regimes is dismissed as self-protective and anti-rigor.

DEBUNKING ASSUMPTION 4

Standards-based approaches have been in place for decades, and their use has been a failure. It has been thirty years since the publication of *A Nation at Risk*,[2] which sparked the effort to reform public schooling by establishing rigorous academic standards and using standardized tests to ensure that students were meeting those standards. Virtually every state developed standards and set up testing regimens that have been in place for more than twenty years.

No Child Left Behind legislation was justified by arguing that standards-based reform had not been successful in reforming schools, so more uniformly rigorous standards, tougher tests, and more severe consequences for not making adequate yearly progress were necessary. Race to the Top initiatives were sold as a remedy for the failed efforts of NCLB; but RttT maintained (even escalated) the use of standards-based accountability as the centerpiece for measuring educational outcomes and motivating (i.e., intimidating) teachers, students, and schools.

There is no evidence that RttT programs, NCLB mandates, or almost thirty years of other standards-based accountability reforms have been effective in improving educational outcomes for children who are not born into middle-class and affluent families in this country.[3] This set of strategies has repeatedly failed to accomplish its purported aims, yet the response from reform diehards is not to abandon these tactics because they are not working. Instead, they push for tougher standards, more tests for more students (including our youngest learners), and threats of more serious consequences for teachers whose students are not mastering the standards.

A rational person might think this repeating pattern of failure would signal the "bottom line" thinkers behind radical education reform that standards-based accountability schemes do not work and ought to be abandoned; but the stubbornness of these folks is stunning. They are like physicians who make faulty diagnoses, then double and redouble the dosage of their off-base prescriptions while their patients continue to suffer. Some of the ways that children, teachers, and schools suffer are explored next.

The negative consequences of standards-based reform for children, teachers, and schools are dismissed or ignored by the purveyors of educational reform. In 2002, an article was published in the *Phi Delta Kappan* that called for resistance to the standards-based reform movement because of ten negative impacts on students, teachers, and schools.[4] The piece was focused on consequences for early childhood education, but it's clear that those negative outcomes have been visited on schooling, teachers, and students across the educational spectrum.

What is interesting, and disturbing, is that more than ten years on, reform advocates continue to dismiss or ignore the consequences of their failed policies. Key elements of the 2002 article are abstracted below:

1. Holding all children to the same academic standard guarantees that some children will face failure and creates potentially debilitating stress for even the most capable students.

2. Teachers experience stress that negatively impacts their relationships with students, effectiveness as instructors, and job satisfaction when they are forced to implement practices that fly in the face of what they know about how children develop and learn.

3. The implementation of standards-based regimes narrows the focus of what is taught and learned in schools so that what is assessed on standardized tests becomes what is covered, leaving far less time for subjects other than language arts and math and almost none for music, art, and physical education.

4. Standards-based accountability reifies the avoidance of punishment as the primary motivation strategy in schools, so children and teachers operate inside a value system that emphasizes the use of fear as a legitimate tool for changing behavior.

5. Implementing standards-based models effectively deprofessionalizes teachers by stripping away autonomy and decision-making power with regard to curriculum, instruction, and evaluation, leaving teachers to

act as technicians who enact the decisions of those who know nothing about the particulars of individual classrooms.

6. In standards-driven schools, children learn that performance on a narrow band of expectations is what counts, and they are systematically denied opportunities to experience the inherent joy of learning for its own sake.

7. The very notion of standardization sets up many children for failure because children are unique individuals, bringing with them an array of backgrounds, experiences, talents, and aptitudes that make expecting them to fit into the preset mold difficult, if not downright cruel.

8. The children and groups who have been marginalized in the past will be further disadvantaged by standards-for-accountability approaches because these children will be expected to perform at even higher levels even though their access to equal opportunity in all parts of their lives remains stagnant.

9. Standards-based approaches benefit reformers because it is a relatively cheap way for them to pretend to be making a difference and then blaming children, teachers, and families when their flawed strategies do not work.

10. The corporate mentality that reformers are applying to the management of schools is changing the ethos of schooling in strikingly negative ways by ignoring the reality that schools are not factories, teachers are not assembly line workers, and students' lives are not commodities that can be mass-produced.

More than ten years later, it is clear that these factors are in play as much (or more) than in 2002.[5] If there are so many negative outcomes from standards-based accountability reforms and they have been shown to be ineffective, why has their influence persisted and expanded? When other explanations are hard to come by, it's always a good idea to follow the money.

The standards-based reform ideology creates a money machine for entities set up to profit from the school reform movement. The advent of the Common Core created an enormous windfall for companies that produce materials associated with standards-based accountability regimes. In the past, testing companies that produced and sold standardized tests to individual states had to put money into developing and field-testing assessment instruments tailored for each state's unique standards. They also had to generate scoring mechanisms that were designed for specific states; so their research and development costs were relatively high.

With all but a handful of states having adopted Common Core, R and D costs are reduced dramatically. Common tests that can be utilized across states to assess Common Core Standards are being developed for fractions of previous costs; scoring techniques that can be applied in multiple states save enormous amounts of money; so profit margins soar. In addition, many states and school districts that previously waited until third grade to start testing and limited the number of grade levels tested are now starting to administer tests at all grade levels, beginning with kindergarten. This means even more money for companies that produce, market, and score standardized tests.

In the same ways, reduced front-end costs improve the profit margins for other enterprises set up to take advantage of the move to adopting and testing Common Core Standards. This includes textbook companies that have been tailoring reading and math texts to fit individual state standards for years. Now, they will be able to generate and publish universal sets of materials, cutting their costs tremendously.

The same is true for all the companies that generate "test-prep" materials that schools purchase to get their students ready for standardized tests. These include mountains of print, computer, and Internet-based materials that can now be focused on Common Core Standards rather than those of individual states. Powerful companies with powerful connections make billions of dollars by keeping standards-based accountability the centerpiece of education reform.

Links among these companies, reform advocates, and political entities that gain from current efforts to alter public schools will be detailed in Part II of this book. For now, it's easy to see that while using standardized testing to ensure accountability masquerades as good pedagogy, it is really just good business.

The purpose of assessment ought to be to improve the teaching-learning process. Along with curriculum and instruction, assessment is the third leg of the education stool. No one with any knowledge of the teaching and learning process argues that assessment is not an essential element of schooling. Assessment is an integral component of the teaching-learning process that helps educators determine if students are learning and shapes what and how teachers need to teach in the future.

However, advocates for high-stakes testing have made it appear that teachers either don't think assessment is important, don't know how to assess their students' progress, or can't be objective about assessing their own effectiveness. This is how reform dependent entrepreneurs rationalize the need for standardized testing schemes for accountability.

As teachers, we need to reclaim our role in assessment. We are the ones who know the special contexts in which we teach. We are the ones who know the students who come through our doors every day. We are the ones who know the content we are teaching. We are the ones who are trained to build a variety of assessment strategies into the fabric of what happens in our schools. We are the ones who need meaningful assessment information to improve the teaching and learning that goes on in our classrooms.

We need to lead the way in reframing the accountability debate so assessment is seen as intimately connected to the teaching we do every day. We need to show those who would take away our professional autonomy that meaningful formative assessment practices created by teachers yield vital information that can never be captured in standardized summative assessment instruments.[6]

Accountability and standards-based testing are so closely linked that these terms are taken to be synonymous by many.[7] It's as if the only way to hold teachers accountable for the learning of their students is to prescribe standards, test kids on the mastery of those standards, and tie teachers' careers to the results of the standardized tests. But there are other ways of thinking about accountability. In Darling-Hammond's words, "Ultimately, accountability is not only about measuring student learning but actually improving it."[8]

Teachers should be accountable for improving student learning. Improving student learning is why we are in this profession. But we need to be able to apply a practice-oriented perspective on assessment, one that makes valid connections among assessment, teaching, and learning.[9] We need to replace the notion of assessment *of* learning with the concept of assessment *for* learning.[10] We need to challenge the assumed primacy of standards-based accountability and make the case for giving us responsibility for using meaningful assessment to inform the ways we improve the learning of our students.

NOTES

1. Harris, P., Smith, B. M., and Harris, J. (2011). *The myths of standardized testing: Why they don't tell you what you think they do.* New York: Rowman and Littlefield.

2. National Commission of Excellence in Education. (1983). *A nation at risk: The imperative for educational reform.* Washington, DC: U.S. Department of Education.

3. Hout, M., and Elliott, S. W. (Eds.). (2011). *Incentives and test-based accountability in education.* Washington, DC: National Academies Press; Jackson, J. (2013). Pivoting from standards- to supports-based reform. *Education Week,* http://www.edweek.org/ew/articles/2013/05/08/30jackson.h32.html

4. Hatch, J. A. (2002). Accountability shovedown: Resisting the standards movement in early childhood education. *Phi Delta Kappan, 83*(6), 457–462.

5. Selected references that support the continued impact of the factors listed include the following: Carter, P. L., and Welner, K. G. (Eds.). (2013). *Closing the opportunity gap: What America must do to give every child an even chance.* New York: Oxford University Press; Kohn, A. (2012). Debunking the case for national standards. In N. Schniedewind percent M. Sapon-Shevin (Eds.), *Educational courage: Resisting the ambush of public education* (pp. 37–41). Boston: Beacon Press; Massachusetts Professors and Researchers. (2013). Massachusetts statement against high-stakes standardized testing, http://matestingstatement.wordpress.com/statement; Leading educators support teacher test boycott. (2013). http://sbloom2.wordpress.com/2013/01/22/leading-educators-support-teacher-test-boycott; Schniedewind, N. (2012). A short history of the ambush of public education. In N. Schniedewind and M. Sapon-Shevin (Eds.), *Educational courage: Resisting the ambush of public education* (pp. 4–22). Boston: Beacon Press; Hout and Elliott. *Incentives and test-based accountability in education;*

Jackson. Pivoting from standards- to supports-based reform; Equity and Excellence Commission (2013). *For each and every child: A strategy for education equity and excellence.* US Department of Education, http://www2.ed.gov/about/bdscomm/list/eec/equity-excellence-commission-report.pdf

6. Black, P., and William, D. (1998). Assessment and classroom learning. *Assessment in Education, 5*(1), 7–74.

7. Graue, E., and Johnson, E. (2011). Reclaiming assessment through accountability that is "just right." *Teachers College Record, 113*(8), 1827–1862.

8. Darling-Hammond, L. (2004). Standards, accountability, and school reform. *Teachers College Record, 106,* 1047–1085. [p. 178]

9. Moss, P., Girard, B., and Haniford, L. (2006). Validity in educational assessment. *Review of Research in Education, 30,* 109–162.

10. Black and William. Assessment and classroom learning.

Chapter Five

Assumption 5

Test scores accurately assess what teachers are teaching and students are learning

THE ASSUMPTION

The entire standards-based accountability movement blows up unless it is assumed that the tests that pervade schooling actually measure what kids are learning. If this assumption were discredited, the lives of hundreds of thousands of teachers and millions of students would change dramatically (as would the cash flow of some of the most powerful corporations in the world). The testing industry depends on this assumption to keep bottom lines fat; and critics of public education rely on it to prove the ineffectiveness of contemporary schools and teachers.

It does not matter that the ways standardized test are being used have been shown to be unfair by social scientists who have examined the impact of such testing. It does not matter that educators have pointed out the inadequacies of such narrowly focused tests to assess the vast landscape of learning that goes on in schoolrooms. It does not matter that testing experts themselves have questioned the efficacy of using standardized tests to make high-stakes decisions that impact the lives of students and teachers. It does not matter that researchers have shown that curriculum content has been drastically narrowed as a result of testing.[1] US schools operate on the assumption that testing provides valid data that reliably tell us all we really need to know about how schools and teachers are doing their jobs.

The impact of operating as if this assumption were true is difficult to exaggerate. If assessment is the tail on the education dog, then it is undeniable that the tail is wagging the dog. In the past, evaluating how well students

29

learned what teachers taught was the purpose of assessment. What counted were curriculum and teaching; assessment was used to get information so that curriculum and teaching could be improved—assessment was the tail.

Now, assessment in the form of standardized, high-stakes tests dominates what gets taught and how it gets covered. The assessment tail drives what gets included in the curriculum. What's tested has become the curriculum of schools, meaning that subject matter areas and content that are not tested get less and less attention all the time.

Preparing kids for tests has taken the place of teaching meaningful content to young people in school. The notion of "teaching to the test" used to be a sign of a bad (even an unethical) teacher; now, it's prescribed practice from kindergarten through high school. The central importance of testing to the radical reform agenda being imposed on public school educators is clear.

The assumption that the tests are doing what they claim is essential to the reformers' case. But what if this is another faulty assumption? What if even those whose job it is to create standardized tests question their current use? What if those who live and work in schools are right that testing does not come close to representing all that is being learned there? What if those who worry about narrowing the curriculum and taking away teachers' professional decision making are lodging a legitimate complaint? What if it can be shown that using tests as we currently do actually hurts children more than it helps? Honest answers to these questions expose the illegitimacy of this assumption.

DEBUNKING ASSUMPTION 5

Multiple issues with standardized tests make their use in high-stakes decisions about children and teachers dubious at best. Reformers rely on test scores to prove their claims that schools are terrible and teachers are doing a lousy job. The best way to attack their assumption that test scores are effective for assessing children's learning and teachers' teaching is to (a) systematically challenge the general efficacy of standardized tests, (b) show the flaws in value-added modeling (VAM) approaches that purport to show teachers' effectiveness year to year, and (c) expose the fallacies of using standardized testing results and VAM measures to make decisions about teachers' value in the classroom.

The case builds on itself: all the flaws in standardized testing contribute to the inadequacies of VAM strategies, and issues with both standardized testing and VAM accentuate the foolishness of using such measures to make decisions about the careers of teachers. Immediately below, issues that call into question the assumed primacy of standardized testing are spelled out. Issues directly associated with standardized testing include the following:

1. Standardized tests reflect cultural bias in question content and answer evaluation. Since their inception, standardized tests have been critiqued for assessing knowledge, language, and ways of thinking that are biased in favor of white, upper- and middle-class test takers.[2] Test producers have made a concerted effort to "scrub" their instruments of materials that put individuals from different cultural backgrounds at a disadvantage, but content selection, item construction, the language of the test, and the scoring of open-ended items continue to privilege "mainstream" students.[3]

2. Standardized tests are constructed in ways that advantage certain groups and disadvantage others. Test makers use complex mathematical formulas to determine which items are selected for inclusion in their instruments. Items are chosen based on their ability to create a spread of scores that allow for comparisons among test takers.

According to assessment expert James Popham, one of the best ways to insure that student performance is spread out is to produce items that are influenced by background factors (e.g., socioeconomic status and inherited academic aptitude) that are already nicely spread out. Popham says this leads to tests that tend to measure "what students bring to school, rather than what they are taught once they get there."[4]

3. Standardized test scores cannot represent the complexity of the teaching and learning process. Even though our society is obsessed with reducing everything to a set of numbers and policy makers want hard "data" to be the basis for their decision making, classroom realities can never be represented with standardized test scores.[5] It seems crazy to imagine that the breadth and depth of what happens between teachers and students can be fairly assessed using tests that measure a very narrow slice of all that could be deemed important and do it at a certain point in time in a sterile, tension-filled setting; yet, we keep on doing it.

Assessment experts have warned for years that using a single test result to make high-stakes decisions about students, teachers, and schools cannot be justified;[6] yet, it keeps on happening. Those of us who actually spend time with students know that test scores are a lame proxy for all that is learned in our classrooms; yet, ignoring common sense, expert opinion, and the voices of experience is a hallmark of reform advocates—so we keep on testing.

4. Standardized tests are incomplete measures of educational outcomes. It turns out that standardized tests do not do a good job of assessing the band of content they purport to cover. Test makers must make decisions about knowledge and behaviors to be assessed as they construct standardized instruments. The tests are too long now, but if items were included for every content domain of interest, testing sessions would be endless. Hence, test developers use content sampling techniques to narrow the item pool. The problem is it is

very difficult to select items that accurately represent the entire domain of knowledge we want students to acquire.[7]

Decisions about what domains of knowledge and skill to assess and what to leave out are arbitrary and may disadvantage students who do poorly on the items selected for inclusion on the test but know content that is not tested. The point is that "test scores are not the same as achievement and . . . the scores represent a sampling of just a small slice of a particular kind of performance on a particular part of a domain of knowledge."[8]

5. Standardized tests underestimate the effects of out-of-school factors on student performance. Scholars who have studied teaching and learning know that out-of-school variables (e.g., family income, family education, family mobility, food insecurity, access to health care, home language) account for 60 percent of the variance in student achievement data. Only 20 percent of variance can be related to in-school factors, and not all of that is tied to teachers' contributions.[9]

Reform advocates ignore this vital information about the limitations of standardized tests. They like to say that educators who point out the devastating impact of outside factors such as poverty are making excuses and not trying hard enough to overcome the learning obstacles children face. The stability of scores across racial and socioeconomic lines clearly show that standardized tests are a better measure of where children live than their aptitude or their teachers' effectiveness. To blame disadvantaged students or their teachers for not trying hard enough is untenable and borders on being mean-spirited.

6. Standardized tests are often ill-matched to the standards and curricula the schools are teaching. As mentioned above, test items are kept or discarded based on how well they spread scores out. When teachers know that certain content is to be tested and prepare their students by covering that content, the likelihood of students getting items related to that content right goes up. If 80 percent or more of students get a question right, it becomes a "bad" item because it won't spread scores enough, and it will be eliminated from future tests.[10]

Educators often complain that nationally normed tests put their students at a disadvantage because what they are teaching is not necessarily being assessed on the standardized tests their students take. Beyond that, even when tests are supposed to be aligned with state standards, the phenomenon described in this section shows how standards and curricula that are emphasized during instruction may systemically be left out of subsequent standardized assessments.

7. Timed portions of standardized tests may distort what students actually know and are capable of doing. When test developers want to increase the score spread on their instruments, one way is to reduce the amount of time students are given to complete the test. Speeding up the test means that students will be less likely to answer items correctly, even if they might have answered correctly if they had more time. [11] Obviously, some students' scores will be deflated by time restrictions, meaning that their scores do not reflect what they actually know and can do.

Students with IEPs are sometimes given more time to complete standardized tests as part of accommodations for their disabilities, but what about the many children with relatively short attention spans who are not qualified for special education? The added pressure of meeting arbitrary time limits, having less time to think, and the impact of short attention spans will negatively (and unfairly) impact the test performance of many students.

8. Scoring of standardized test items is often done by temporary workers with no professional knowledge of or experience in education settings. Giant testing companies such as Pearson have contracts with individual states and school districts to provide standardized testing services, from creating the tests to scoring them. The scoring includes assessing open-ended items that cannot be scored with computers. To find graders for the open-ended responses, these companies advertise for test graders on Craigslist and other media outlets.

Graders need no experience in education and are paid by the hour. The graders are trained to make quick decisions about the rightness or wrongness of particular items based on criteria provided by the testing company. [12] Millions of dollars are spent to pay temps to make decisions that have a major impact on the lives of students and teachers. It's hard to make a good guess about the error rates associated with this practice, but they must be considerable.

9. Standardized tests are not objective. Reform advocates claim that educators are incapable of reaching sound conclusions about how well their students are learning because teachers rely on subjective judgments. What we need, it's argued, are objective measures of student performance—like those provided by standardized tests. In fact, accountability systems based on standardized testing are human creations that are rife with subjectivity, political influence, and technical judgments. [13]

Test items are created by human beings, often freelancers who submit as many items as they can generate in hopes that some will be accepted (and paid for). Test development committees are made up of people who establish test specifications that set out the content and form of the exam. Item development committees are folks who apply the specifications to the selection and creation of items. Panels of content specialists are often assigned the task of setting passing scores and proficiency levels, and deciding what consti-tutes grade-level work. All of these activities are accomplished by human beings making subjective judgments all along the test development and inter-pretation process.[14]

> 10. Standardized tests include measurement error that is often ignored as re-sults are reported. Standardized tests do not produce "objective," unambiguous data because measurement error is a fact of life in all efforts of this kind. All measurement tools have built-in error, and good ones report margins of error, which are plus or minus a few percentage points on a well-designed instru-ment.[15] Problems arise when a particular score is used to make decisions about passing, proficiency, and program placement or to assess teaching effec-tiveness without regard for margins of error.

If there is a margin of error of plus or minus 3 percent and one student is one point above the cut score and another is one point below, their scores are statistically indistinguishable; yet, the first student would make the grade and the other not. This lack of precision can have dramatic consequences for individual students. Averaging such scores compounds the problem, but this is what happens when standardized test data are used to assess student per-formance across classrooms, schools, systems, and even states and countries.

> 11. High-stakes standardized testing regimes lead to strategies designed to "game the system" rather than facilitate learning. The stakes are so high and the consequences so devastating that some schools and teachers have adopted tactics that attempt to increase test scores without improving student learning. We have all heard of cheating scandals in various cities, where school person-nel have been accused of altering answer sheets to make it appear that student performance is better than it actually is. Such activities are morally wrong and professionally inexcusable.

Other practices, such as focusing instructional attention on "bubble kids" (i.e., those who are close to proficiency levels) at the expense of other stu-dents who have slim chance of making the grade or those who are well above the cutoffs are sanctioned and even encouraged in some systems.[16] It can be argued that the intensive test preparation that now goes on in most schools is another form of "gaming the system," that is, utilizing practices that might improve test scores without improving the educational experience of stu-dents.[17] Such practices make interpreting test results for accountability diffi-cult and are a sad commentary on the state of education in the age of account-ability.

Value-added models that rely on standardized test data are flawed in several important ways. Value-added modeling involves a complex set of statistical techniques that attempt to isolate a teacher's impact on his or her students' test scores from year to year, while controlling for other measurable factors such as student and school characteristics.[18] The value-added notion comes from the assumption that a teacher should add at least one year's worth of progress when his or her students' test scores are converted to grade equivalents each year.

If the average growth score of a teacher's class of students is higher than one year, the teacher is thought to have added value; if the scores show less than a year's growth, the teacher has not been effective. In spite of the many concerns about standardized tests in general (listed above) and VAM in particular (addressed below), states and school districts across the nation are turning to VAM approaches. Issues specific to VAM include the following:

> 1. VAM cannot adequately account for non-teacher effects on student perfor-
> mance on standardized tests. Standardized tests were not designed to assess
> teacher effectiveness, so accurate conclusions about teachers' impact on stu-
> dent test performance is not possible.[19] Researchers who have studied the
> application of value-added models have consistently warned against their use
> to estimate teacher contributions to student growth as measured on standard-
> ized tests. They caution that VAM outcomes are descriptive at best and that
> causal inferences about teacher or school effects are not warranted.[20]

Reviewing the research literature related to using test scores to evaluate teachers, a group of distinguished scholars concluded that "[a] number of factors have been found to have strong influences on student learning gains, aside from the teachers to whom their scores would be attached."[21] Some of the factors these experts identified are:

- influences of other teachers (past and current);
- tutors or instructional specialists available in some schools;
- quality of curriculum materials;
- class size;
- pull-out and scheduling practices;
- school attendance;
- out-of-school learning experiences at home and in communities;
- parent support for learning;
- family resources;
- student health;
- family mobility;
- the influence of neighborhood peers and classmates;
- summer learning loss for many students; and
- the nonrandom placement of English learners, special education students, and low-income students.[22]

Despite efforts by VAM developers to account for non-teacher variables, experts warn that value-added models are not equipped to isolate teacher effects from factors such as these and others (e.g., student motivation and prior knowledge).[23]

> 2. Since students are not randomly assigned to teachers and because the numbers of students in teachers' classrooms are small, VAM outputs are subject to significant error. Researchers who have tracked state data across several years have found that VAM estimates for middle and high school teachers are unreliable from year to year because of the nonrandom placement of students with particular teachers.[24]

Students are typically tracked in middle and high school, which means that certain teachers work with higher-achieving students while others teach students in the lower tracks. The research shows that value-added modeling does not adequately account for the sorting bias that these nonrandom placements bring into play, systematically leaving those who teach more remedial classes with lower value-added scores than those who taught higher-level students.[25]

Similar issues exist in the placement of students at the elementary level. Certain teachers are more frequently assigned to classes that include students with disabilities, students whose home language is not English, or students who live in poverty; studies have shown that VAM cannot control completely for the influence of these nonrandom sorting factors.[26] The impact of these errors is compounded because of the small numbers associated with generating VAM estimates for individual teachers.

Teacher scores in New York, for example, can be based on assessment data from as few as ten students, meaning that the likelihood of distortion is sky-high.[27] As assessment experts have concluded, "When there are small numbers of test-takers, a few students who are distracted during the test, or who are having a 'bad' day when the tests are administered, can skew the average score considerably."[28] More on error and VAM follows.

> 3. The effects of measurement error in standardized tests are compounded in VAM formulas. As noted above, measurement error that is built into any standardized test is virtually ignored as a student's test scores are used to make educational decisions. Averaging the scores from an individual teacher's class for VAM multiplies the potential impact of measurement error, meaning that the VAM outputs obscure as much information as they reveal.[29] Worse, since VAM calculations depend on having data for multiple years, teachers' scores are affected by measurement error on at least two different tests, making VAM results even less reliable than a single test score.[30]

> 4. VAM measures are highly unstable from year to year. It is reasonable to expect that a teacher who is effective one year would be effective the next year, but studies of VAM implementation show great variability in teachers' scores from year to year. One study of score instability showed that only a

third of teachers who were ranked in the top 20 percent one year were in the top scoring group the next year, and another third moved all the way to the bottom 40 percent.[31]

In fact, VAM estimates have proven to be unstable when different VAM statistical models are used on the same teacher data and when the same models are applied to different classes taught by the same teachers.[32] In other studies, where different tests were administered to assess student learning of the same content, teacher VAM scores again varied widely.[33]

There is broad agreement among independent entities that have systematically analyzed the efficacy of using VAM approaches that technical problems seriously threaten the validity of interpretations based on VAM data.[34] The Board on Testing and Assessment of the National Research Council summarized: "VAM estimates of teacher effectiveness should not be used to make operational decisions because such estimates are far too unstable to be considered fair and reliable."[35]

The American Statistical Association, which has no political interest in education or the reform movement, issued a report in 2014 that warned, "Ranking teachers by their VAM scores can have unintended consequences that reduce quality." They continue, "This is not saying that teachers have little effect on students, but that variation among teachers accounts for a small part of the variation in scores."

5. VAM scores may be significantly influenced by previous teachers, creating a "halo" or "pitchfork" effect. Longitudinal analyses of VAM data reveal that the positive effects of being placed with highly effective teachers can persist for years, as can the impact of being in the class of a low-performing teacher.[36] The impact on the validity of gain scores for teachers who have students in either of these groups is obvious. The presence of a halo or pitchfork effect adds to the many sources of distortion that make the use of VAM approaches essentially useless for assessing teaching quality.

6. Data fed into VAM formulas may be inaccurate. As teachers' value-added scores have been released to the public in places like New York City and Los Angeles, numerous examples of inaccuracies in the data reported have come to light. In New York, for example, data were reported on teachers who were on leave, data were not included for teachers who had taught for years, teachers' scores were reported for subjects for which they had no or very little teaching responsibility, and scores for students who had spent only a few weeks in a particular teacher's classroom were included in the VAM calculations.[37]

What is most troublesome is that inevitable errors like these are routinely ignored by the states and school systems that use VAM data to make judgments about teachers and schools. School officials are fine with assuming

that VAM scores are accurate and valid, even in the face of obvious evidence
to the contrary.

*Evaluating teachers using student test scores, including VAM outputs, has
been shown to be full of problems.* We have explored general issues tied to
standardized testing and issues specific to VAM. The next subsection brings
these two elements together and lays out problems directly related to evaluating teachers based on students' standardized test scores and value-added
models. These issues include the following:

> 1. Standardized tests were created to assess individual performance, not that of
> teachers, schools, districts, or states. Even those who produce standardized
> achievement tests think it's a bad idea to use them to assess teacher effective-
> ness. The tests are designed for a specific purpose: to measure the performance
> of individual students.

These instruments are not designed for assessing teachers and schools, and
they are not capable of doing so. Professors and researchers from Massachusetts have called for an end to the use of standardized tests to evaluate
teachers, noting that "because the tests are not designed to determine teacher
effectiveness, no accurate conclusions can be drawn about an individual
teacher from her students' test scores."[38]

Given all of the problems with the tests themselves and the VAM approaches described above, it seems doubly absurd to think that tools that are
ill-suited for the job of measuring individual student achievement should be
applied to the even more complex task of assessing teacher performance. In
the words of test experts, "If you add up all the problems the tests exhibit for
individual students and create a teacher or school score, the original problems won't magically disappear."[39]

> 2. Single measures such as standardized test or VAM results should not be
> given so much weight in assessing an activity as complex as teaching. We
> have seen that student achievement growth as measured by VAM is flawed at
> best; yet to qualify for Race to the Top incentives, states across the nation
> agreed to utilize student growth data as part of their teacher evaluation models.
> In the face of all the issues associated with this approach, these states signed
> on for making teacher evaluations at least 40 percent dependent on student
> growth.

It is presumed that observation and other measures will make up the remaining 60 percent or less. Even if it turns out to be less than half of the total
evaluation, because student growth data will vary more (for all the reasons
above) than other kinds of data brought to the teacher evaluation formula,
student growth will have an unwarranted impact on outcomes and become
the primary tipping point for decisions regarding teacher effectiveness.[40]

Giving so much weight to measures that are of questionable validity and reliability is unsupportable and unfair.

> 3. Using arbitrary and rigid cutoff scores to classify teachers is statistically indefensible. As teacher evaluation schemes have rolled out in response to RttT funding requirements, states have assigned arbitrary cutoffs to determine teacher effectiveness. For example, a score of 25 percent or below might be considered ineffective; 26 to 75 percent effective; and 76 percent and higher highly effective. As noted above, a teacher's placement in these categories will depend largely on student growth data. The problem is that because of measurement error built into the evaluation system, making distinctions among teachers who are close to the cut scores is completely unjustified. [41]

Studies of classification errors in teacher evaluation systems like those described here show that the likelihood that a teacher will be misclassified is high. One study estimated that the chances of an "average" teacher being classified as "significantly worse than average" based on VAM data was as high as 35 percent. [42] Reform advocates and their allies in Washington and state legislatures want to get tough and make sure teachers are assessed based on how much value they add to their students' achievement; but assigning teachers to arbitrary categories based on error-ridden data says more about the reformers' real goals than about the quality of teaching they claim to be assessing.

Other studies show weak or no relationship between VAM measures and teaching quality. Researchers have shown that teachers' performance on assessments of their ability to cover content, align their teaching with appropriate standards, or deliver high-quality instruction are not related to their VAM outcomes. [43] So what has been understood to be effective teaching may have little or no relation to teachers' VAM rankings. Summarizing such studies, one critic concludes, "So value-added models can be messy. They can be 'noisy.' They can easily be misconstrued." [44]

> 4. The impact of student effort is left out of formulas designed to assess teacher performance. Anyone who has ever observed students during the administration of a standardized test knows that different children have different reactions to the testing situation. No matter how much the school and its teachers encourage students to do their best, some will react to the test by freezing up, shutting down, or making "Christmas trees" on their scan forms. Some are just too nervous to do a credible job of showing what they have learned; some would rather not try than face the reality of trying and failing; others are fine with sabotaging a system they see as unfair and oppressive.

All of these realities keep test scores from showing what children have learned, and none reflect what or how well teachers have taught. All this points to the fact that in the current reform climate, teachers are being evaluated based on how well their students do on tests, not on how well educators actually teach. As the old axiom goes, "Attendance is compulsory; learning is optional."[45]

Current teacher evaluation models place teachers, no matter their competence in the classroom, in the position of depending on student effort during the year and during the test administration period to determine their fate. For this and all the reasons outlined in this section, the assumption that test scores accurately assess what teachers are teaching and students are learning in school must be challenged. We need to confront reformers who have placed all their accountability eggs in this basket and let them know the myriad reasons why their eggs are rotten and the basket is falling apart.

NOTES

1. Board on Testing and Assessment, National Academy of Sciences. (2009, October 5). Report to the U.S. Department of Education on the Race to the Top Fund, http://www.nap.edu/catalog.php?record_id=12780

2. Gould, S. J. (1996). *The mismeasure of man.* New York: W. W. Norton.

3. Kumashiro, K. K. (2012). *Bad teacher: How blaming teachers distorts the bigger picture.* New York: Teachers College Press.

4. Popham, W. J. (2011). Misunderstood measurement mallets. In P. Harris, B. M. Smith and J. Harris, *The myths of standardized testing: Why they don't tell you what you think they do.* New York: Rowman and Littlefield. [p. 21]

5. Kohn, A. (2012, September 19). Schooling beyond measure. *Education Week,* http://www.alfiekohn.org/teaching/edweek/sbm.htm

6. American Educational Research Association. (2000, July). Position statement on high-stakes testing in pre-k–12 education, http://www.aera.net/PositionStatementonHighStakesTesting/tabid/11083/Default.aspx

7. Harris, Smith, and Harris, *The myths of standardized testing.*

8. Harris, Smith and Harris. *The myths of standardized testing.* [p. 53]

9. Berliner, D. C. (2014). Effects of inequality and poverty vs. teachers and schooling of America's youth. *Teachers College Record, 116*(1), 1–14.

10. Popham, W. J. (2001). *Truth in testing.* Alexandria, VA: Association for Supervision and Curriculum Development.

11. Harris, Smith and Harris. *The myths of standardized testing.*

12. Ravitch, D. (2013, January 29). The biggest testing scandal of all. *Diane Ravitch's Blog,* http://dianeravitch.net/2013/01/29/the-biggest-testing-scandal-of-all/

13. Smith, M. L. (2003). *Political spectacle and the fate of American schools.* New York: Routledge.

14. Harris, Smith and Harris. *The myths of standardized testing.*

15. Harris, Smith and Harris. *The myths of standardized testing.*

16. Booher-Jennings, J. (2005). Below the bubble: "Educational triage" and the Texas accountability system. *American Educational Research Journal, 42*(2), 231–268.

17. Graue, E., and Johnson, E. (2011). Reclaiming assessment through accountability that is "just right." *Teachers College Record, 113*(8), 1827–1862; Harris, Smith and Harris. *The myths of standardized testing.*

18. Di Carlo, M. (2012). How to use value-added measures right. *Educational Leadership, 70*(3), 38–42.

19. Massachusetts Professors and Researchers (2013). Statement against high-stakes testing, matestingstatement.wordpress.com/statement/

20. Rubin, D. B., Stuart, E. A., and Zanutto, E. L. (2004). A potential outcomes view of value-added assessment in education. *Journal of Educational and Behavioral Statistics, 29*(1), 103–116.

21. Baker, E. L., Barton, P. E., Darling-Hammond, L., Haertel, E., Ladd, H. F., Linn, R. L., Ravitch, D., Rothstein, R., Shavelson, R. J., and Shepard, L. A. (2010). Problems with the use of student test scores to evaluate teachers. Washington, DC: Economic Policy Institute. [p. 2]

22. Baker, et al. Problems with the use of test scores to evaluate teachers.

23. Goodwin, B., and Miller, K. (2012). Use caution with value-added measures. *Educational Leadership, 70*(3), 80–81.

24. Harris, D. N., and Anderson, A. A. (2012, November). Bias in public sector worker performance monitoring: Theory and empirical evidence from middle school teachers. Paper presented at the Annual Meeting of the Association for Public Policy and Management, Baltimore, MD; Jackson, C. K. (2012, January). Teacher quality at the high school level: The importance of accounting for tracks. National Bureau of Economic Research, http://www.nber.org/papers/w17722

25. Sawchuk, S. (2012, October 23). "'Value added'" measures at the secondary level questioned. *Education Week*, http://www.edweek.org/ew/articles/2012/10/24/09tracking_ep.h32.html

26. Rothstein, J. (2009). Student sorting and bias in value-added estimation: Selection of observables and unobservables. *Education Finance and Policy, 4*(4), 537–571; Baker, et al. Problems with the use of test scores.

27. Goodwin and Miller. (2012). Use caution with value-added measures.

28. Baker, et al. Problems with the use of test scores to evaluate teachers. [p. 9]

29. Harris, Smith and Harris. *The myths of standardized testing.*

30. Baker, et al. Problems with the use of test scores to evaluate teachers.

31. Schochet, P.Z., and Chiang, H.S. (2010). Error rates in measuring teacher and school performance based on student test score gains. Institute for Education Sciences, U.S. Department of Education, http://ies.ed.gov/ncee/pubs/20104004/pdf/20104004.pdf

32. Baker, B. D., Oluwole, J., and Green, P. C. III. (2013) The legal consequences of mandating high stakes decisions based on low quality information: Teacher evaluation in the race-to-the-top era. *Education Policy Analysis Archives, 21*(5), 1–65; Baker, et al. Problems with the use of test scores.

33. Papay, J. (2011). Different tests, different answers: The stability of teacher value-added assessments. *American Educational Research Journal, 48*(1), 163–193.

34. Horn, J., and Wilburn, D. (2013). *The mismeasure of education.* Charlotte, NC: Information Age Publishing.

35. Board on Testing and Assessment, National Academy of Sciences. (2009, October 5). Report to the U.S. Department of Education on the Race to the Top Fund, http://www.nap.edu/catalog.php?record_id=12780

36. Sanders, W. L., and Horn, S. P. (1998). Research from the Tennessee Value-Added Assessment System (TVASS) database: Implications for educational evaluation and research. *Journal of Personnel Evaluation in Education, 12*(3), 247–256.

37. Goodwin and Miller. (2012). Use caution with value-added measures.

38. Massachusetts Professors and Researchers. (2013). Statement against high-stakes testing, http://matestingstatement.wordpress.com/statement/

39. Harris, Smith and Harris. *The myths of standardized testing.* [p. 41]

40. Baker, B. D. (2012, April 19). The toxic trifecta: Bad measurement and evolving teacher evaluation policies. *School Finance 101*, http://schoolfinance101.wordpress.com/2012/04/19/the-toxic-trifecta-bad-measurement-evolving-teacher-evaluation-policies/

41. Baker. The toxic trifecta.

42. Schochet and Chiang. Error rates in measuring teacher and school performance.

43. Polikoff, M. S., and Porter, A. C. (2014). Instructional alignment as a measure of teaching quality. *Education Evaluation and Policy Analysis*, http://epa.sagepub.com/content/early/2014/04/11/0162373714531851

44. Yettick, H. (2014, May 13). Studies highlight complexities of using value-added measures. *Education Week*, http://www.edweek.org/ew/articles/2014/05/13/32value-add.h33.html [p. 3]

45. Harris, Smith and Harris. *The myths of standardized testing.* [p. 41]

Chapter Six

Assumption 6

Public schools need to be privatized

THE ASSUMPTION

If your goal is to corporatize education, then you need to generate private alternatives to the public schools you have worked so hard to demonize. For-profit and parochial private schools have been in place for a long time, so an easy way to take funds out of the public sector and move them into private enterprise is through voucher systems. The promise of programs that handed parents chits they could spend on private education for their children spawned an explosion of investment in for-profit educational enterprises.

Business interests saw the education market as an opportunity to pocket billions of dollars. But voucher systems have not been as widely adopted as expected, and those that have been tried have had spotty success. Voucher initiatives are not dead, but the plan B for the business interests that want to take over schooling in America is to put more of their efforts into the charter school movement.

Based on the assumptions of failed schools outlined above, monies are taken from public schools and given to private entities that set up charter schools not burdened with all the bureaucratic restrictions of public educa-tion. The same business interests that were ready to feed off voucher pro-grams are the ones that promote, finance, and profit from the charter school movement.

In order for this multibillion-dollar business plan to work, the public has to assume that charter schools are better than public schools. Given their success in selling the assumption that public schools are abject failures, it should be no problem for the powerful entities involved to get everyone to assume that charters are better than the "government schools" they are designed to replace.

For starters, it is argued that when charter schools are freed from the red tape and overregulation of public schools, they will be much more efficient and effective. Sound business principles will be used to make decisions in charter schools, and they will not be burdened with barriers like teacher tenure or collective bargaining as they establish working conditions at their places of business. Further, if they can set their own criteria for who gets to enroll and who does not, what gets taught and how, and how long the school day and school year last, charter schools are bound to be better than the public schools now in place.[1]

DEBUNKING ASSUMPTION 6

Voucher programs have failed to produce significant positive change for children and families. Public school reform advocates rely on the logic of free-market economics to make their case. Based largely on economic theories applied to education by influential libertarian thinkers of the mid to late twentieth century (e.g., Milton Friedman[2] and John Chubb and Terry Moe[3]), contemporary reformers argue that market-based principles are needed to dramatically reshape the dismal educational landscape.

Three basic privatization strategies have been tried in various forms: (1) voucher programs that dole out chits, which parents can use to enroll their children in private schools; (2) privately managed schools, in which private interests contract with school systems to take over the management of certain schools; and (3) charter schools that are set up when organizations are granted autonomy by public school authorities, allowing them to operate without many of the restrictions placed on public schools. None of these approaches to privatizing public schooling has had a consistently positive impact on the quality of education it provides.[4]

In theory, voucher programs apply free-market economic principles by creating competition among public and private alternatives. It was thought that if parents were given vouchers that they could use to shop around for high-quality schools, then schools would improve to the point where they would attract voucher dollars or fail and be shut down. Vouchers never gained the political traction necessary to see widespread use.

In the 1950s and 1960s, vouchers were seen as a way to subsidize white flight from public schools that were forced to desegregate as a result of *Brown v. Board of Education.*[5] Later, community groups, teacher unions, and policy makers fought against voucher strategies because vouchers made it possible to shift public funding for education into the hands of private institutions, including church-related private schools; and they advantaged even more those families who could already afford private education for their children, while poor families were offered meager benefits and were once again left with few or no real choices.[6]

More recent attempts have focused on providing vouchers specifically to families living in communities served by substandard schools, making it possible for students to access private schools, parochial schools included. Legislatures in states like Indiana, Florida, Wisconsin, and Alabama have passed voucher plans of some sort into law in recent years.[7] Big-city systems like Milwaukee, Cleveland, Chicago, and the District of Columbia have included vouchers along with other market-based options in their attempts to implement educational reform. Perhaps, the most dramatic application of this approach occurred post hurricane, when "Katrina Vouchers" were issued in New Orleans.

Evidence shows that reform efforts that include vouchers have not been effective in significantly improving schools. For example, using vouchers in New Orleans resulted in further inequality, as impoverished children were sent to schools with even fewer resources than prior to the devastation.[8]

Across numerous studies of voucher plans implemented in a variety of places, there is no evidence of a clear advantage for students in voucher schools over those in regular public schools. Even when there are apparently slight improvements of voucher students' performance, close analyses show that students with the largest academic needs are those likely to receive the least benefit from changing to a voucher school.[9]

The pattern is that students in districts that have implemented voucher plans continue to lag well behind when compared with state, national, and international samples. Vouchers have not produced the promised results. Overall, the academic performance of students in voucher schools and the schools they leave is statistically the same; and both groups continue to underperform in relation to students across the spectrum.[10]

Private management of schools has proven to be a failed strategy. The 1990s saw the advent of a number of educational management organizations (EMOs) that were formed by entrepreneurs who saw the potential for huge profits in taking over the management of public schools. Most prominent among these were Chris Whittle, who founded Edison Schools, and John Golle, who created Education Alternatives, Inc (EAI). These and other venture capitalists saw a vast potential for turning a profit by offering to run schools more efficiently than the public school personnel in place at the time; and they were able to attract investments from wealthy backers and Wall Street speculators to start up their enterprises.[11]

These entrepreneurs sold their services as a way for school districts to improve the outputs of low-performing schools by paying the EMOs directly and giving managers the autonomy to run the schools in such a way as to cut costs, increase efficiency, and improve production (i.e., student performance). Early adopters included large city school systems such as Baltimore, Hartford, and Dade County for EAI, while Edison took on schools in cities like Dallas, San Francisco, New York, and Philadelphia.

The expected success of EMOs did not materialize in terms of finances or school improvement. These businesses were put together and marketed to investors during a time when it was expected that voucher legislation would be successful and parents would be flocking to EMOs with their education chits in hand. When that did not happen, the projected numbers of schools that these companies planned to bring under their control dropped dramatically. Because EMOs were banking on an economy-of-scale business model (Whittle told investors Edison would be the next Wal-Mart), the smaller numbers made potential profit estimates and stock values plummet.[12]

As time passed and data became available on the academic performance of privately managed schools, systems did not renew contracts with EMOs, further damaging their credibility and profitability.[13] While companies like Edison reported positive academic gains for students in their programs, outside researchers questioned those findings, concluding that EMO students perform no better and no worse than students in comparable schools.[14]

For example, in 2007, the Rand Corporation published a study of the impact of EMOs on student achievement in Philadelphia schools. The report concluded that "despite additional per-pupil resources, privately operated schools did not produce average increases in student achievement that were any larger than those seen in the rest of the district."[15]

While some companies went bankrupt as a result of the unforeseen difficulties of applying business management models to school contexts, others just shifted their focus from managing schools outright to supplying products and services to schools such as after-school programs, professional development, consulting services, tracking programs, tutoring services, test development, and test preparation.[16] In addition, the rise of charter schools opened another entrepreneurial door to private companies that were unsuccessful at managing public schools.

Charter schools have failed to be the panacea that reform advocates banked on. Charter schools are the next iteration of efforts to privatize public schooling. They represent the centerpiece of reform advocates' current table setting. Charter schools are those that have been established by groups (e.g., parents, nonprofit agencies, for-profit management groups, organizations, or businesses) that want to create an alternative to existing public schools.

Charters are contracts negotiated between these groups and the state or local agencies that have been given the authority to review applications and grant school charters. Charter schools receive public money at approximately the same level as public schools in the districts in which they operate, and their contracts have to specify the ways the charter schools will operate, what their curricula will include, and how assessment will be accomplished.[17]

A wide array of charter schools has sprung up in various parts of the United States. The concept of charter schools dates to the progressive ideals of Albert Shanker, president to the American Federation of Teachers in the 1980s. Shanker envisioned groups of teachers establishing schools within schools to address the needs of unsuccessful students—a vision that never came to life. [18]

The rationale for the charter schools that evolved was that by freeing schools from the rigid regulations thought to hamper innovation in public schools, charters could develop approaches that would show public schools how to improve. However, these outcomes never materialized. [19]

Today, some schools have been established by parent groups and church-related organizations; but the vast majority of charters are run by educational maintenance organizations. For-profit charters and charters run by nonprofit EMOs with backing from wealthy individuals and reform-minded philanthropic organizations are ubiquitous in large urban systems with a history of subpar academic performance—places like Chicago, Philadelphia, New Orleans, Denver, Los Angeles, and New York City. [20]

A great deal of controversy is associated with the charter school movement, especially those charter programs designed to serve traditionally underserved urban communities. While advocates point to the successes of some high-visibility charter programs, critics are quick to challenge the purported outcomes of even the most successful programs at the same time they are documenting the failures and abuses of many charter enterprises.

Perhaps the best-known charter organization is the Knowledge is Power Program (KIPP), which was started by two Teach for America alumni in 1994. Most KIPP schools are middle-grades schools characterized by longer school days, Saturday classes, and extra time in the summer. Potential students are selected via a lottery system, and students, parents, and teachers sign contracts that specify explicit responsibilities for each.

KIPP schools have an impressive record of improving academic performance, and there are currently over eighty KIPP schools across the country. [21] However, critics have several concerns about KIPP and costs associated with the apparent success of its programs, including the following:

1. Like other charter programs, KIPP has been accused of "skimming" the cream of the crop when it comes to selecting students for admission. It is claimed that improved academic success can be attributed to selecting (and retaining) higher-performing students who come from highly motivated families, leaving those with less promise in the public schools to which KIPP is favorably compared. [22]

2. Per-pupil expenditures for KIPP and other charter programs are often higher than comparable local schools. Much of this extra funding

comes from private and philanthropic sources, which masks the advantages these schools have over those to which they are compared.[23]

3. Attrition rates are higher in KIPP and other charter programs among both students and teachers when compared to local public schools. Students who are unwilling or unable to keep up with the rigorous schedule required are forced to leave the program, and teachers often leave after a short stay because of the intensity and duration of workplace expectations.[24]

4. Critics worry that programs like KIPP create an environment that teaches children to be compliant and follow the rules rather than giving them opportunities to think for themselves and develop their own sources of motivation.[25] Others worry that such schools isolate children from their home communities, imposing a "pedagogy of surveillance" on them, making students good test takers but limiting their capacities to become empathetic, thoughtful citizens.[26]

5. KIPP schools are not good models of what's possible because it would be impossible to duplicate the special circumstances that characterize KIPP schools (and others like them) in the public school sector. For example, public schools must enroll all comers and cannot limit their student bodies to top students who are willing to submit themselves to longer school days, weeks, and years. Further, the public schools across the board cannot rely on the support of generous donors to supplement their limited budgets, and they would have great difficulty attracting and keeping staff in such schools.

These are issues that taint the very best charter schools, but other serious problems exist in the broader charter school context. Some of the most troublesome issues associated with establishing charter schools (especially in big-city systems) are outlined below:

> 1. The quality of charters runs from very good to deplorable. KIPP schools and others like them are well managed and have carefully designed programs; but, many schools that have received charters are run by individuals with no idea of how to educate students and no interest in anything but reducing expenditures on curriculum, materials, staff, and facilities so that profits can be maximized.[27]

Online charters are among the worst, with more than 70 percent being identified as academically unacceptable in 2012.[28] Some charters purvey alternatives to traditional science teaching regarding topics such as evolution and global warming.[29] Even charter school advocates acknowledge the wide disparity in charter quality, noting that while many are doing great things, some of the worst and "flakiest" schools are charter schools.[30]

2. Charter schools as a group enroll fewer students with disabilities, fewer English language learners, and fewer students who qualify for free and reduced lunch. This gives such schools an unfair advantage when the performance of their students is used to demonstrate their superiority to traditional public schools that end up serving the students that charters reject. This unfairness is multiplied when charters invoke policies that allow them to remove students who don't meet expectations for behavior or academic performance. [31]

3. Charter schools expel students at a much higher rate than do public schools. Charter schools have the freedom to operate independently of the rules that govern public schools with regard to suspending and expelling students. For example, the *Washington Post* examined 2011–2012 records from District of Columbia charter and public schools and found that DC charter schools expelled students at a rate seventy-two times higher than DC public schools, meaning that the expelled charter students had nowhere to go except back to the public schools they left in order to attend a charter—public schools that are legally bound to take them in. [32]

4. Research reveals that charter schools and other school choice alternatives are effectively resegregating US schools. Many charter programs are designed to target specific racial or ethnic groups, which by definition increases segregation. Further, as noted above, beyond race, ethnicity, and income, the selective admissions built into school choice programs result in increased segregation for special education and language minority students. [33]

5. Many big-city systems are closing large numbers of community public schools and sending students to proprietary charter schools. In places like Chicago, New York City, Philadelphia, and Washington, DC, scores of traditional public schools are being closed in communities that primarily serve students from poverty and minority backgrounds. In New Orleans, the remaining public schools in the Recovery School District were replaced by charters in 2014. [34]

Reformers claim that urban schools are failing and financially unsustainable at the same time they lobby for passing out millions of dollars to support the expansion of unproven charter schools in the same districts. Critics see these reactions as one element of a larger effort to privatize public schooling, without regard for the wishes of parents or communities. [35]

Looking at the academic performance of charter schools in comparison to regular public schools, it is clear that charters have not proven to be the game changer that advocates had hoped for. One comprehensive study completed by Stanford University reported that only 17 percent of charter schools had outcomes that bested traditional public schools; 37 percent were worse than comparison schools; and 46 percent showed no significant difference in academic performance. [36]

These findings parallel the conclusions of careful syntheses of research that have looked at the relative academic success of charter schools in comparison to traditional public schools that serve similar communities.[37] Even when ignoring the issues of selection bias described above (charters often select and retain only the top students), there is no evidence that charter schools do a significantly better job of improving the academic performance of their students. If this is the case for voucher programs, private management of public schools, and charter schools, it begs the question of why reform advocates continue to support their proliferation.

The school choice movement is a thin smokescreen for privatizing public education in the United States. "School choice" became the preferred term when advocates for changing schools based on free-market economic principles saw that they needed to implement their policies via the back door. Reformers saw resistance to their ideas when they were presented too baldly, so they appropriated the discourse of progressive educators who were alarmed by the pervasive gaps in achievement between children of privilege and those with fewer resources and opportunities.

Libertarian ideologues saw the struggling schools in large urban centers as places where they could gain a foothold on implementing their policies. Ironically, under the guise of giving "choice" to parents in underserved communities, wealthy and powerful entrepreneurial reformers advanced their own financial and political interests, while leaving behind those they claim to be helping.

As is clear, the choices offered have not worked. Vouchers, EMOs, and charter schools are simply strategies for shifting public control of education to the hands of private interests. It does not matter that these approaches have not had the dramatic positive impact they promised; money, power, and ideology are the engines that are driving education reform efforts, and evidence that market-based reform initiatives are not working is ignored.

NOTES

1. Fabricant, M., and Fine, M. (2012). *Charter schools and the corporate makeover of public education: What's at stake?* New York: Teachers College Press.
2. Friedman, M. (1955). The role of government in education. In R. A. Solo (Ed.), *Economics and the public interest* (pp. 123–144). New Brunswick, NJ: Rutgers University Press; Friedman, M., and Friedman, R. D. (1980). *Free to choose: A personal statement.* New York: Harcourt.
3. Chubb, J. E., and Moe, T. M. (1990). *Politics, markets, and America's schools.* Washington, DC: Brookings Institution Press.
4. For a concise history of the "school choice" movement, see Ravitch, D. (2010). *The death and life of the great American school system: How testing and choice are undermining education.* New York: Perseus Books. [pp. 113–147]
5. Ravitch. *The death and life of the great American school system.*
6. Fabricant and Fine. *Charter schools and the corporate makeover of public education.*

7. Cavanagh, S. (2012). Vouchers gain foothold among state, local Democrats. *Education Week*, http://www.edweek.org/ew/articles/2012/09/19/04vouchers_ep.h32.html

8. Kumashiro, K. K. (2012). *Bad teacher: How blaming teachers distorts the bigger picture*. New York: Teachers College Press.

9. Ravitch. *The death and life of the great American school system*.

10. Ravitch. *The death and life of the great American school system*.

11. Bracey, G. W. (2003). *What you should know about the war against American public schools*. Boston: Allyn and Bacon; Burch, P. (2009). *Hidden markets: The new education privatization*. New York: Routledge.

12. Weil, D. (2009). *Charter school movement: History, politics, policies, economics and effectiveness*. Amenia, NY: Grey House Publishing.

13. Bracey. *What you should know about the war against American public schools*.

14. Saltman, K. J. (2005). *The Edison Schools*. New York: Routledge; Weil. *Charter school movement*.

15. Gill, B., Zimmer, R., Christman, J., and Blanc, S. (2007). *State takeover, school restructuring, private management, and student achievement in Philadelphia*. The Rand Corporation, http://www.rand.org/content/dam/rand/pubs/monographs/2007/RAND_MG533.pdf

16. Burch. *Hidden Markets*.

17. Weil. *Charter school movement*.

18. Ravitch. *The death and life of the great American school system*.

19. Schniedewind, N. (2012). A short history of the ambush of public education. In N. Schniedewind and M. Sapon-Shevin (Eds.), *Educational courage: Resisting the ambush of public education* (pp. 4–22). Boston: Beacon Press.

20. Kumashiro. *Bad teacher*.

21. Ravitch. *The death and life of the great American school system*.

22. Goodman, J. F. (2013). Charter management organizations and the regulated environment: Is it worth the price? *Educational Researcher*, *42*(2), 89–96, Ravitch. *The death and life of the great American school system*.

23. Baker, B., Libby, D., and Wiley, K. (2012). *Comparing charter school and local public district financial resources in New York, Ohio, and Texas*. Boulder: University of Colorado, National Education Policy Center; Goodman. Charter management organizations and the regulated environment.

24. Miron, G., Urschel, J. L., and Saxton, J. (2011). What makes KIPP work? A study of student characteristics attribution and school finance. New York: Teachers College, National Center for the Study of Privatization in Education; Goodman. Charter management organizations and the regulated environment.

25. Goodman. Charter management organizations and the regulated environment.

26. Hartman, A. (2013, February 17). Teach for America's hidden curriculum. *Jacobin Magazine*, https://www.jacobinmag.com/2011/12/teach-for-america/; Kuhn, J. (2012). Contextual accountability. *The Educator's Room*, http://theeducatorsroom.com/2012/09/contextual-accountability

27. Bracey. *What you should know about the war against American public schools*.

28. Berliner, D. C., and Glass, G. V. (2014). *50 myths and lies that threaten America's public schools: The real crisis in education*. New York: Teachers College Press.

29. Hiltzig, M. (2014, January 21). Creationism again stalks the classroom. *Los Angeles Times*, http://www.latimes.com/business/hiltzik/la-fi-mh-creationism-20140121-story.html

30. Finn, C. E. (2004, August 19). No August break in charter-land. *Education Gadfly*, http://www.edexcellence.net/commentary/education-gadfly-weekly/2004/august-19/No-August-break-in-charter-land.html

31. Fabricant and Fine. *Charter schools and the corporate makeover of public education*; Schniedewind. A short history of the ambush of public education.

32. Brown, E. (2013, January 5). D. C. charter schools expel students at far higher rates than traditional public schools. *The Washington Post*, http://articles.washingtonpost.com/2013-01-05/local/36208283_1_charter-advocates-charter-schools-traditional-public-schools

33. Rotberg, I. C. (2014). Charter schools and the risk of increased segregation. *Phi Delta Kappan*, *95*(5). 26–30.

34. Layton, L. (2014, May 28). In New Orleans, major school district closes traditional public schools for good. *Washington Post*, http://www.washingtonpost.com/local/education/in-new-orleans-traditional-public-schools-close-for-good/2014/05/28/ae4f5724-e5de-11e3-8f90-73e071f3d637_story.html

35. Bryant, J. (2013, February 2). The inconvenient truth of education 'reform.' *Campaign for America's Future*, http://blog.ourfuture.org/20130202/the-inconvenient-truth-of-education-reform

36. Stanford University Center for Research on Education Outcomes. (2009, June). *Multiple choice: Charter school performance in 16 states*, http://credo.stanford.edu/reports/MULTI-PLE_CHOICE_CREDO.pdf

37. Two such syntheses are reported in Fabricant and Fine. *Charter schools and the corporate makeover of public education*; Ravitch. *The death and life of the great American school system.*

Chapter Seven

Assumption 7

Business models have direct application to education

THE ASSUMPTION

It's easy to see the pervasive influence this assumption has on any discussion of educational reform. Educators' (especially teachers') ways of thinking about improving education are ignored or dismissed by the movers and shakers behind educational reform.

What's needed are hard-nosed approaches that have been successful in building and sustaining big businesses. What's needed are leaders (from Washington to state departments of education to local schools) who understand and are committed to applying sound business principles to the administration of schools. What's needed are policies and practices that improve the productivity of schools as measured by objective outcome data.[1] Who could argue with that?

Tied to the assumption that a corporate approach is needed to fix a failed public system is the surety of reform advocates that the values, principles, and practices of those who have been responsible for providing public education are suspect. Those of us who have made careers out of trying to learn as much as possible and do as much as possible to provide educational experiences that enhance the life chances of every student who enters our doors are not just being ignored; we are being told that our way of being is the problem.

Educators' commitment to finding ways to make learning meaningful and relevant turns out to be a liability in schools driven by market-based forces. Our concern that students need be treated as complex individuals who deserve a broad exposure to more than easily measured basic reading and math skills turns out to be a sign of inefficiency in corporatized schools. Our desire to be treated as professionals who are capable of making informed decisions about curriculum, instruction, and evaluation is seen as insubordination by forces that know more than we do about what makes schools successful enterprises.

Success in America is measured by how much money and power individuals and corporations have acquired. Teachers and other education professionals are paid notoriously small salaries, and our influence on decision making that directly impacts our future is almost nil.

"Successful" individuals are pulling the strings on educational reform. Virtually all of these individuals have direct ties to big business; and the ones with the most impact are heavily influenced by the logic of free-market capitalist tenets. The upshot is that the current educational reform agenda assumes that models from the world of business are the only way to turn around our failing schools.

DEBUNKING ASSUMPTION 7

The application of business models to bringing about social changes, such as reforming schools, does not work. It's not just education that the billionaire businesspeople who are bankrolling the current education reform movement want to change. Michael Edwards has chronicled the rise of "philanthrocapitalism," through which individuals who have become super wealthy via their business dealings set up philanthropies that grant money to organizations contingent on those organizations being willing to apply business thinking and market forces to solve social problems.

Edwards identifies Bill Gates as the archetype philanthrocapitalist because his foundation has given so much money to address a variety of social causes, including education reform. But Edwards makes the case that business approaches alone cannot work to bring about meaningful social change, and some key elements of his argument are abstracted below:

1. Claims that markets should regulate themselves, that business will protect the public good, and that nonprofits should learn efficiency, transparency, and accountability from Wall Street have been shown to be disastrous, causing the economic crash of 2008; so why should these claims be applied to the public sector?
2. Social change happens when people work together using all means possible to achieve their ends; so why would we expect business principles like price competition, profit motive, and supply-chain control to bring about the compassion and solidarity necessary for meaningful change?

3. Business has a part to play in encouraging social change; but why would we expect business leaders to be the only legitimate actors in a very complex drama?
4. That business thinking can save the world is a convenient myth; so why do we celebrate rich and famous individuals who distract us from the reality that all of us need to work together to make a difference?
5. Much of the wealth of the philanthrocapitalists has been accrued without paying anywhere near their fair share of taxes; so why should we not expect that if businesses paid taxes at the same rate as the rest of us then government would have money to address the areas taken on by the super wealthy?
6. Many philanthrocapitalists were and are famously ruthless in running their corporations, creating monopolies, exploiting their workers, and subverting policies meant to regulate them; so why would we expect them to provide the moral leadership necessary to bring about social change?
7. The increasing concentration of wealth and power among a few individuals is unhealthy for a democratic society; so why should decisions about the production of goods and services like health and education for the many become the province of a select few?
8. Philanthrocapitalists see capitalism as the solution to problems that capitalism created; so why would we expect different results when free-market principles are applied in the public sector?
9. Businesses measure success in terms of profit margins, size, growth, and market share; so why would we attempt to apply these sterile metrics to the assessment of complex human endeavors such as education?[2]

Edwards is talking about the inability of wealthy philanthrocapitalists to impact social change across the board. He shows that applying business principles to social change efforts does not and will not work. Edwards's analysis has direct application to education. For all the reasons listed above (and below), market-based solutions will not change education in positive ways; but it's hard to underestimate the reach of those who want to privatize schooling.

The business metaphor is inadequate for describing the depth and complexity of education. Metaphors are tricky rhetorical devices. They can help reveal connections between phenomena in ways that are hard to observe directly; but they can also mask dissonances, leaving out contrasts that mark significant differences in the phenomena under investigation. Applying the business metaphor to education leaves out more than it reveals. As Bill Ayers points out,

The dominant metaphor in education today posits schools as businesses, teachers as workers, students as products and commodities, and it leads to rather simple thinking that school closings and privatizing the public space are natural events, relentless standardized test-and-punish regimes are sensible, zero tolerance a reasonable proxy for justice—this is what true believers call "reform."[3]

Thinking of schools as businesses means that goals such as helping students develop their own interests and potentials, generating an appreciation for the value of lifelong learning, or becoming well-rounded citizens get overshadowed by aims such as getting a job or getting into college to get a better job.

It's not that being qualified and ready to work is not an appropriate goal; the concern is that any intrinsic value in education is being replaced by narrow concerns for accomplishing the "measurables" dictated by the business model. The business model emphasizes competition, profit, and individual success, leaving out desirable attributes like cooperation, community, and working for the greater good.

Race to the Top initiatives set up a competition for resources based on state and district willingness to accept business-driven policies such as performance pay and charter schools.[4] The outcome of competition is both winners and losers, which business thinkers see as a natural and fitting result; but real teachers, children, and families lose when change is based on arbitrary competitive criteria. As Jim Burns summarizes,

Through our devotion to the ethos of competition rampant in education policy, we have actually entered into a race to the bottom illustrated by our treatment of teachers, the worship of simplistic metrics of success, the reduction of curriculum to the attainment of quantifiable outcomes, and an oversimplified conceptualization of teaching.[5]

Applying the business metaphor means that practices designed to increase profits (no matter the human consequences) are being utilized in schools. Examples from business that are being applied to education include closing plants that don't meet annual production goals, hiring less qualified workers to replace those making more money, taking away or reducing worker benefits, getting rid of or reducing the power of organized labor, and systematically firing the lowest-performing managers annually in an attempt to clear out those who are not meeting productivity criteria.[6]

A school is not a factory, and children are not widgets moving along an assembly line. Schools are complex human endeavors that will never be able to fit into the mold prescribed by outside interests who cannot imagine a world not run on bottom-line business principles.

A focus on test scores as the product of the schooling enterprise leaves out more of what is important than it includes. The many flaws in standardized tests and their use in assessing students and teachers are detailed above. The interest here is in critiquing the use of tests as a proxy for business outcomes. Business is results oriented, and business thinkers believe that educators are soft because they do not want to provide hard evidence for the products of their work.[7]

Within the business model of education, test scores are taken to be the hard evidence of productivity. As one concerned educator points out,

> What gets measured gets done, and make no mistake: "reformers" understand that full well. In fact, they count on it. They see data, not children. For the corporate reformers, test data constitute the bottom-line profits that they watch.[8]

Applying data-driven business models to education means that students are being trained to take tests rather than being truly educated. Academic subjects not tested receive far less attention and instructional time than those that are. Life-enhancing areas like art, music, physical education, philosophy, foreign languages, and literature are shortchanged or left out of the curriculum entirely.

It does not matter that bodies as distinguished as the National Academy of Sciences have found that testing regimes designed to increase performance in education do not provide an adequate measure of desired educational outcomes.[9] Business leaders, testing companies, and the media continue to insist that without rigorous testing, American public schools cannot be trusted to educate our children.[10]

Education has been reduced to numbers, and this fact is not lost on the students experiencing it. Students are judged and judge themselves based on abstract, arbitrary measurements. The intrinsic value of learning and sheer joy of learning cannot be quantified, so students do not experience them. They internalize the materialistic values on which contemporary schooling is based and become alienated from learning itself. Worse, if the product of schooling is a meaningless score, then achieving that score at any cost, including cheating, lying, and deception, can be easily justified.[11] This looks a lot like how big business operates and leads to the next talking point.

The individuals bankrolling education reform based on business practices are not the best models of the kinds of moral behavior we hope to instill in children. Most of the movers and shakers behind applying business principles to schooling have gained their wealth and influence by creating giant corporations based on practices that are the antithesis of the kinds of ethical thinking we want children to internalize. Super-wealthy individuals and families have accrued their fortunes via besting their competitors by any means possible, reducing their costs no matter the consequences for their workers or the communities in which they are located, and avoiding the payment of taxes as much as possible.

Like the robber barons of the industrial revolution, the current crop of super successful business tycoons have set up foundations to "give back" a small portion of what they have gained from exploiting the capitalist winner-take-all system. Both iterations hearken back to the ruthless lords, mayors, and bishops of medieval times who tried to buy their way into heaven by building churches, cathedrals, or hospitals, using the resources they extorted from peasants living in abject poverty under their rule.

The point here is simple: the business practices that have made it possible for a few individuals to acquire so much wealth and power provide a lousy example of ethical behavior, so why would we adopt the practices these same individuals are foisting on schools? Education can and should be organized and delivered in ways that teach principles such as individual integrity, social commitment, and the inherent value of learning.

Students can learn to see that there are purposes for school-based education that go beyond passing the test to get to the next grade level, get a job, or get into college. Business moguls are neither good models of the kinds of human beings we want our children to become nor good architects of the kinds of schools we need in our society.

NOTES

1. Ravitch, D. (2010). *The death and life of the great American school system: How testing and choice are undermining education.* New York: Perseus Books.

2. Edwards, M. (2010). *Small change: Why business won't save the world.* San Francisco: Berrett-Koehler.

3. Ayers, B. (2012). Another world is possible/Another education is necessary. In N. Schniedewind and M. Sapon-Shevin (Eds.), *Educational courage: Resisting the ambush of public education* (pp. 194–200). Boston: Beacon Press. [pp. 194–195]

4. McClung, M. (2013). Repurposing education—Instead of new standards, how about an old one: The civic standard. *Phi Delta Kappan, 94*(8), 37–39.

5. Burns, J. (2014, May 5). Our impoverished view of teacher education. *Teachers College Record*, http//:www.tcrecord.org

6. Camins, A. H. (2012, November 7). A call for President Obama to change course in education. *Washington Post*, http://www.washingtonpost.com/blogs/answer-sheet/wp/2012/11/07/a-call-for-president-obama-to-change-course-on-education

7. Ohanian, S., and Brady, M. (2012, September 7). Outing ACT: Test-and-punish doesn't educate, but it's profitable for testing companies. *Truthout*, http://truth-out.org/news/item/11361-outing-act-test-and-punish-doesnt-educate-but-is-profitable-for-testing-companies

8. Burris, C. (2013, March 4). Principal: I was naïve about Common Core. Washington Post, http://www.washingtonpost.com/blogs/answer-sheet/wp/2013/03/04/principal-i-was-naive-about-common-core [p. 3]

9. Hout, M., and Elliott, S. W. (Eds). (2011). *Incentives and test-based accountability in education.* National Academy of Sciences, http://216.78.200.159/RandD/Other/Incentives%20and%20Test-Based%20Accountabillity%20-%20NAS.pdf

10. Ohanian and Brady, Outing ACT.

11. Hvolbek, R. (2012, February 6). The end of education. *Teachers College Record*, http://www.tcrecord.org/Content.asp?ContentID=16686

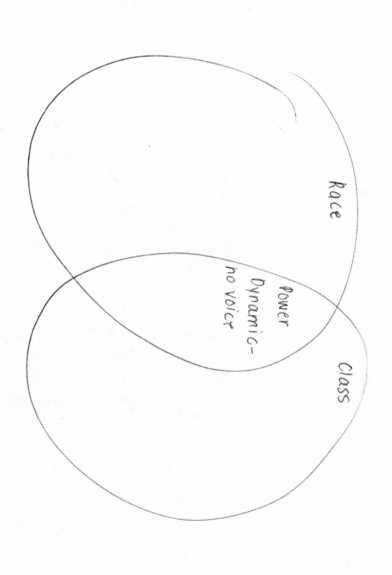

Race

Power
Dynamic-
no voice

Class

Chapter Eight

Assumption 8

Teachers' unions are a major reason why schools are so bad

THE ASSUMPTION

The free-market ideologues who want to privatize public schools are anti-union by definition. They are savvy enough to know that unions provide a way for individuals to unite in a common cause and speak with a common voice. The history of union activity in the United States is a narrative of individuals forming associations that provided protection from unfair labor practices.

Keeping the unions weak or nonexistent has historically made a small number of folks super rich, while large numbers of workers barely survived. From the robber barons of the early twentieth century to the union-busting legislatures of today, organized labor has been a target for destruction. Teachers' unions are no exception.

There was a time when the Democratic Party supported unions in general and teachers' unions in particular. The National Education Association and the American Federation of Teachers (the two major organizations representing American teachers) continue to support Democratic candidates. However, the contemporary rhetoric (unions have been called everything from "roaches" to "terrorists"[1]) from both parties almost always includes references to limiting the influence of teachers' unions.

It's assumed that the existence of unions is a major contributing factor in the failure of public education. Ineffective teachers and poor teaching practices are shielded by unions. Tenure and other means of protecting inept teachers are the stock-and-trade of teachers' unions. Unions always try to

61

block changes that would require teachers to work harder. And unions have consistently opposed educational voucher systems and for-profit charter schools.

Based on this spurious logic, educational entrepreneurs and reformers from across the political spectrum are sure that we need to get rid of unions to implement the kinds of sweeping changes they have in mind.[2] As they build their cases for dismantling public education, limiting the collective bargaining rights of teachers is essential.

As with the other assumptions, raising the negative impact of teacher unionization to the taken-for-granted level refuels the momentum for privatizing schools. If the goal is to apply free-market capitalist principles to schooling, then unions (the traditional counterbalance to exploitive labor practices) are clearly in the way. Recent events in states like Wisconsin, Ohio, and Tennessee are clear examples of the close link between the educational reform agenda and the attack on teachers' collective bargaining rights.

DEBUNKING ASSUMPTION 8

Advocates portray unions as villains who resist education reform at every turn. It is no surprise that the business leaders who are funding and profiting from the education reform movement are anti-union. The history of efforts by big business and industry to destroy organized labor is long and frightening. What may surprise some is the venom advocates spew on unions as they try to make the case for school reform. But their attacks on unions make sense when you consider that individual teachers have almost no power to resist their own degradation.

Unions have been the only means by which workers in all domains have had a collective voice in the past. Reformers understand that fact, and they know that by reducing or eliminating teachers' unions they are effectively stifling the resistance of those who seek to defend their profession and preserve public schooling in the United States.

The powerful forces behind radical education reform have created the impression in the media and in the minds of the public that teachers' unions (i.e., the American Federation of Teachers [AFT] and the National Education Association [NEA]) block attempts to reform at every turn. Reform advocates' favorite ploy is to claim that these labor organizations protect ineffective teachers, making it virtually impossible to fire them. This is a straw man argument that distorts collective bargaining agreements designed to protect teachers from being arbitrarily dismissed without due process, turning them into evidence of the unions' unwillingness to support school improvement at any cost.

The discussion below outlines these and other positions staked out by anti-union reform advocates and contrasts them with the perspectives of teachers' unions on issues that are intimately tied to contemporary education reform:

1. Collective bargaining

Reform advocates see collective bargaining as a major roadblock to their objective to privatize schooling, and they have found willing allies among conservative state legislatures across the nation. Unions have a long history of supporting Democratic candidates, and Republican- and Tea Party–controlled state governments would like to see unions of any kind diminished in size and importance. Education reformers have helped create a perfect storm for attacking teachers' unions, funding the campaigns of political allies and helping draft legislation that greatly reduces the collective bargaining rights of teachers.[3]

Reformers propagate the impression that the collective bargaining agreements negotiated between schools and teachers' unions effectively hamstring their efforts to bring about the radical changes they want to see. Their solution is to do everything in their power to limit or eliminate collective bargaining rights for teachers—to get rid of teachers' unions or, at the least, significantly reduce their influence.

Teachers' unions see collective bargaining as a fundamental right. The Wagner Act of 1935 was the hard-earned outcome of long and bloody conflicts between workers and those who exploited them. The Wagner Act was designed to protect workers who organize themselves into unions to speak with a collective voice, and that collective voice is being silenced in states like Wisconsin, Tennessee, and Ohio.[4] Contracts that are negotiated between teachers' unions and school systems via the collective bargaining process spell out all the elements addressed below.

Yes, reform advocates don't like collective bargaining agreements because reformers want to shift American education to schools that set their own salary schedules, determine their own benefit schemes, define their own hiring and firing policies, and establish their own working conditions (e.g., class size, working hours, yearly calendar, curriculum). It's no coincidence that almost 90 percent of charter schools are nonunion.[5] Without collective bargaining rights, teachers are stripped of their mutual capacity to mount a defense against those who assume teachers are inept and schools need to be operated as for-profit enterprises.

2. Salaries

Reform advocates see teacher salaries as the most costly element on the debit side of their ledgers. If the goal is to maximize profits, then reducing salaries is the place where costs can be cut most dramatically. Unions have negotiated contracts that set up uniform salary schedules with step raises based on years of experience and education, and reformers see these as targets of opportunity. Reform advocates argue that competition is eliminated when salary scales are uniform and step raises (however meager) are doled out based on making it through one more year.

Reformers want merit pay approaches based on teacher performance (largely determined by student test scores) installed to take the place of the current system. They want to eliminate giving teachers monetary credit for earning advanced degrees and for years of experience. They want the flexibility to establish charter schools that set their own salary schedules without interference from unionized teachers.

Unions see teacher salaries as low in relation to the professional responsibilities of the job and in comparison to the compensation patterns of other occupations that require similar preparation. They know that already depressed teacher pay has lost ground as a result of the latest economic downturns, and they see it as their job to support teachers by resisting reform efforts that flatten teacher pay schedules and implement merit pay schemes.

Unfortunately for teachers, legislation in many states has stripped unions of their influence, and as a result, teachers' abilities to make a decent wage are under constant threat. Radical reformers and their conservative political allies have pushed through state policies that significantly reduce the wage-earning capacities of lifetime teachers, making it less attractive for high-quality teachers to stay in the profession. One critic summarizes that these policies are designed to create a situation in which "[t]eachers will be trained quickly, paid little, and burn out, thus maintaining the revolving door in education. Low salaries will help cut costs."[6]

Careful studies of the effects of merit pay systems on the performance of workers in general[7] and teachers in particular[8] show clearly that such schemes simply do not work. In fact, performance pay is as likely to undermine the intrinsic rewards of teaching as it is to increase extrinsic motivation.[9] But research findings like these are ignored as reformers work hard to link teacher pay (and continued employment) to teacher productivity as measured via student test scores.

3. Benefits

Reform advocates see benefits through the same eyes as they see teacher salaries: benefits are expensive, and they keep operating costs high. When state budgets are tight, as they have been of late, insurance costs, retirement benefits, and even pension funds for public employees, especially teachers, are favored targets for those who want to privatize public enterprises like schooling.

Again, conservative legislators and those who pull their strings blame unions for creating the fiscal problems that plague their state governments, creating the impression that unionized teachers are receiving benefits that are causing a disproportionate drain on state monies. Further, charter school operators avoid hiring teachers affiliated with unions because operating expenses can be kept low and profits high by providing minimal insurance and retirement benefits.

Unions see the threats to teacher benefits as a place to take a stand on behalf of current and retired educators. Unions want teacher benefits to be comparable to what workers in the private sector receive, they want the benefits already earned by teachers to be safe from those who would raid funds that retired teachers depend on for economic survival, and they want teachers to be able to join unions in order to protect themselves from being denied equitable insurance and retirement benefits.

Teacher unionization is under attack in the current political environment, and the unions' hard work in negotiating contracts that provide basic security for teachers is being systematically eroded. This is a sign of success to the movers and shakers behind radical education reform.

4. Job security

Reform advocates see tenure and other forms of job protection for teachers as a major roadblock to school improvement. They portray teacher tenure as making it impossible or at least exceedingly difficult to get rid of ineffective teachers. They see unions' support for protecting teachers from being fired as evidence for why unions need to be harnessed or done away with altogether. Some have baldly asserted that US education would be best served if we simply fired the 5 to 10 percent of teachers with the lowest test scores. [10]

The concept of improving schools by getting rid of low-performing teachers takes shape on a large scale in the form of massive school closings in several urban centers. Based on the logic behind the policies of No Child Left Behind, thousands of teachers are being fired or reassigned as hundreds of "failing" public schools in poor and minority communities are being closed (to be, not surprisingly, replaced with charter schools).

In various forms in various states, reformers have advanced legislation to eliminate tenure, weaken tenure protections, lengthen the time it takes to earn tenure, increase the requirements for tenure, build in regular reviews of tenure once is it awarded, and tie tenure directly to student performance on test scores.[11] It is clear that attacking union support for measures that provide job security for teachers is a high priority for education reformers.

In June 2014, a California court ruled that state tenure laws were unconstitutional in a case brought by students with the support of education reform advocates and a high-powered law firm. Secretary of Education Arne Duncan wasted no time supporting the ruling and proclaiming that teacher tenure in the United States is a "broken status quo."[12] It can be expected that education reformers in more states will be pushing the courts to diminish teachers' job security via legal attacks on teacher tenure.

Unions see tenure as the only tool teachers have for protecting themselves from being fired arbitrarily based on the personal or political whims of their administrative superiors. Tenure does not guarantee continued employment. In spite of how it is portrayed by reformers, tenure does not protect teachers from being fired for incompetence, misconduct, or insubordination. It is designed to guarantee that teachers cannot be fired without due process.

Teachers' unions see the job security of their members eroding because of the reasons outlined throughout this section. They also acknowledge that some teachers are not fulfilling their responsibilities in the classroom and should be let go. However, they point out that merely firing teachers who do not score well on value-added assessments or closing large numbers of low-performing schools are strategies that are bound to fail.

If the goal is really to improve teacher quality, then other approaches make more sense than taking away protections that keep teachers from being fired for political, economic, or capricious reasons. Some approaches to improving teacher quality via proactive means that could be supported by unions include:

- reducing the assignment of teachers to subjects they are not prepared to teach;
- providing more support for new teachers;
- providing more effective interventions for teachers who are struggling;
- increasing opportunities for teacher collaboration;
- providing more time for lesson planning and preparation;
- reducing class sizes; and
- doing more to retain the many good teachers who leave the profession every year.[13]

5. Career development

Reform advocates see teachers as technicians who need only minimal training and experience to implement prepackaged ("teacher-proof") curricula designed to improve test scores. They don't see the value of comprehensive teacher preparation, ongoing professional development, or studying for advanced degrees. They make contracts with school systems that stipulate the hiring of Teach for America recruits with six weeks of preparation in place of experienced teachers or new teachers who have completed four- or five-year teacher preparation programs. [14]

With their corporate partners, they package and promote professional development programs focused on implementing test preparation materials sold by those same corporate partners. [15] Further, education reformers have taken the position that advanced degrees in education do not make teachers more effective, so they are lobbying state legislatures to take away increases in teachers' pay based on continuing university preparation. [16]

Unions see teachers as professionals who deserve to have the same opportunities for career development as their counterparts in other fields. As in all other professions, unions want entry into the profession to be based on the completion of university-based, fully accredited initial preparation programs. As in all other professions, they want experience to be recognized and rewarded across an individual's career. As in all other professions, they want the additional knowledge and expertise gained through advanced study to be valued.

Reform advocates do not count teachers as professionals, and their disdain for teachers is evident in how they think about teachers' career trajectories. The business model that reform advocates want to apply to education emphasizes keeping costs down, and it takes money to attract and keep a professional workforce. It's easy to see why deprofessionalizing teachers is a central goal of the education reform movement and why unions are trying hard to resist.

6. Working conditions

Reform advocates see teaching as easy work with short hours and lots of built-in vacation time. As they establish charter schools, they want to set their own class sizes and working hours. Many of their charters feature larger classes, more hours in the school day, Saturday classes, and more teaching days per year. [17] Of course, managers don't want unions representing the teachers in their charters because unions protect teachers from working conditions that are unfair, not adequately compensated, or harmful to teachers and students.

Reform advocates are also lobbying to legislate these kinds of changes in existing public schools. They play on manufactured public perceptions that teachers are just not working hard enough because unions have negotiated soft conditions of employment; so as reformers minimize the power of unions, they seek to increase the workload for teachers.

Unions see teaching as complex and difficult professional work that is undertaken under stressful conditions. They are not automatically opposed to changing school calendars or workdays, but they want teachers to have a voice in negotiating working conditions that make sense for their own and their students' well-being. They want elements other than efficiency and cost savings to be factored into decisions about class size and working hours. If teachers are expected to do more for longer periods of time, unions want them to be compensated fairly for the additional work.

Unions want to establish working conditions that will encourage teachers to stay in the profession rather than being burned out after two or three years of incredibly difficult work. Students benefit when class sizes are small and their teachers' work lives are sane and secure. Unions and the teachers they represent want an improved workplace because they know that "good working conditions are good teaching conditions, and good teaching conditions are good learning conditions."[18]

8. Job performance

Reform advocates see student test scores as the most accurate measure of teachers' job performance. They define effective teachers as those who improve their students' standardized test scores, and they see unions as the obstacle to getting rid of ineffective teachers and hiring effective ones. In education reformers' perfect world, effective teachers would be rewarded for their higher test scores and ineffective teachers would be let go. Higher pay for effective teachers would help attract and retain outstanding teachers, while ineffective teachers would be fired, and schools would be improved.

As Diane Ravitch has summarized, "The answer to the problem of ineffective teachers, or so goes the argument, is to eliminate the teachers' unions or at least render them toothless, then fire the teachers whose students get low scores."[19] The problem for teachers and their unions is that emphasizing student test scores in evaluating teacher job performance was codified in requirements for receiving Race to the Top monies from the Obama administration. A make-or-break element in successful RttT proposals has been to guarantee that a major portion of teachers' evaluations will be based on standardized test data; and states across the nation now mandate this provision for assessing teacher performance.

Unions see student test scores as a flawed and insufficient tool for assessing teachers' effectiveness in the classroom. Using arguments that parallel those detailed earlier in this book, unions protest that test-based evaluations are unreliable, inaccurate, and unfair. They resist attempts to reduce the complex, multilayered activities of teaching to measures that focus on only one dimension of teachers' work—and do that poorly at best.

Teachers and the unions that represent them are not against being evaluated on their job performance; but teachers want their evaluations to reflect their actual capacities to positively impact the lives of their students. They want job performance assessments to be based on performance, not just a numerical outcome that distorts what the students have learned and can't begin to represent what teachers have taught or how well they taught it. They ask how it can be national education policy to base the assessment of teacher performance on test-driven evaluation schemes that have been clearly shown to be unstable, unreliable, and unfairly biased against teachers working in certain contexts.[20]

Efforts to limit teachers' union power and influence have been well organized, heavily financed, and very successful. Even though no evidence exists that links the presence of teachers' unions to negative academic outcomes, reformers have mounted a dramatic and successful negative public relations campaign targeting teachers' unions. Those who seek to dismantle public education understand the central importance of incapacitating teachers' unions to achieving the changes they seek.

Reformers' market-driven ambitions would be thwarted if teachers were able to speak with a collective voice to protect their hard-earned rights. Michael Fabricant and Michelle Fine state it clearly: "So, let us make no mistake, part of the intention of the public-sector decision makers and their allies is to reduce the power of the one institution that can contest the exercise of unilateral managerial power—unions."[21]

Successful efforts to reduce union influence are dramatically evident in places like Wisconsin and Tennessee. In 2011, the nation watched as teachers, workers from other unions, and a few brave legislators fought unsuccessfully to block bills in Wisconsin that effectively stripped teachers of their collective bargaining rights. As a result of this legislation, teachers and staff were let go, retirement and health benefits were reduced, and the establishment of working conditions was turned over to local school boards—all leading to large numbers of Wisconsin teacher retirements and resignations.[22]

While receiving far less media attention, Tennessee teachers' unions suffered a similar fate. Stripping teachers of their union representation created the opening for a landslide of reform initiatives designed to: increase support for charter schools; do away with teacher tenure; establish a teacher evaluation system that makes it possible for teachers to be graded on the test performance of students they have never seen; make it possible to get rid of (take away the licenses of) teachers who have consecutive years of low value-added scores; and replace the existing salary schedule with one that builds in merit pay, reduces step raises from seventeen to four, and does not reward teachers for earning advanced degrees.[23]

In chapter 11, the network of powerful individuals and institutions that provide economic and political support for the reform agenda, including the attack on teachers' unions, will be described in detail. The point here is to signal the effectiveness of reformers' efforts (in places as different as Wisconsin and Tennessee) to reduce the power of unions and advance their radical change agenda.

The propaganda efforts of the reformers and their political allies portray unions as the bad guys in their dramatic (mis)representations of public schooling. In fact, the idea that unions somehow hurt communities, schools, and students is not supported by empirical evidence. As they rail against unions, reformers conveniently forget that countries with test scores that they admire have heavily unionized teaching forces (e.g., Finland, where 98 percent of teachers and principals belong to unions).

Reform proponents also never mention that the states with the highest standardized test scores are located in the North, where there is the highest union participation among teachers. In contrast, the lowest-scoring states are concentrated in the South, where unions represent the fewest teachers.[24]

Unions are willing to support change that actually improves the educational opportunities of America's children. They want to work with parents to save local public schools from being closed so that entrepreneurs can profit from setting up charter schools in their communities. They want to provide representation for the hundreds of thousands of public school teachers whose professional integrity is being questioned and whose careers are under attack.

If reformers have their way, collective bargaining and collective representation for teachers will disappear. As David Berliner and Gene Glass point out,

> Those leading the anti-union movement are often the same group of people who see money to be made from public education and will do whatever it takes to make profits from public education—especially a nonunionized profession of educators.[25]

NOTES

1. Berliner, D. C., and Glass, G. V. (2014). *50 myths and lies that threaten America's public schools: The real crisis in education.* New York: Teachers College Press. [p. 78]

2. Schniedewind, N. (2012). A short history of the ambush of public education. In N. Schniedewind and M. Sapon-Shevin (Eds.), *Educational courage: Resisting the ambush of public education* (pp. 4–22). Boston: Beacon Press.

3. Guo, J. (2013, July 8). Reforming Michelle Rhee. *New Republic,* http://www.newrepublic.com/article/113204/michelle-rhee-tennessee-studentsfirst-floods-school-races

4. Luhby, T. (2011, February 22). Teachers under attack. *CNNMoney,* http://money.cnn.com/2011/02/22/news/economy/Governors_teachers_jobs_union/index.htm

5. Ravitch, D. (2012, September 10). Two visions for Chicago's schools. *New York Review of Books,* http://www.nybooks.com/blogs/nyrblog/2012/sep/12/two-visions-chicagos-schools/

6. Schniedewind. A short history of the ambush of public education. [p. 19]

7. Gabor, A. (2010, September 22). Why pay incentives are destined to fail. *Education Week,* 30(4), 24, 28.

8. Springer, M., Ballou, D., Hamilton, L., Le, V., Lockwood, J., McCaffrey, D., Pepper, M., and Stecher, B. (2010). *Teacher pay for performance: Experimental evidence from the project on incentives in teaching.* Nashville, TN: National Center on Performance Initiatives at Vanderbilt University.

9. Firestone, W. H. (2014). Teacher evaluation policy and conflicting theories of motivation. *Educational Researcher, 43*(2), 100–107.

10. Hanushek, E. (2009). Teacher deselection. In D. Goldhaber and J. Hannaway (Eds.), *Creating a new teaching profession* (pp. 163–180). Washington, DC: Urban Institute Press.

11. Greenblatt, A. (2010, April 29). Is teacher tenure still necessary? *National Public Radio*, http://www.npr.org/templates/story/story.php?storyId=126349435

12. Staiti, C. (2014, June 16). Teacher tenure is a 'broken status quo,' Secretary Duncan says. *Bloomberg*, http://www.bloomberg.com/news/2014-06-16/teacher-tenure-is-a-broken-status-quo-secretary-duncan-says.html

13. Gerson, J. (2012). The neoliberal agenda and the response of teachers unions. In W. H. Watkins (Ed.), *The assault on public education: Confronting the politics of corporate school reform* (pp. 97–124). New York: Teachers College Press.

14. Strauss, V. (2013, August 29). How Teach for America recruits get preference for teaching jobs. *The Washington Post*, http://www.washingtonpost.com/blogs/answer-sheet/wp/2013/08/29/how-teach-for-america-recruits-get-preference-for-teaching-jobs

15. Ohanian, S., and Brady, M. (2012, September 7). Outing ACT: Test-and-punish doesn't educate, but it's profitable for testing companies. *Truthout*, http://truth-out.org/news/item/11361-outing-act-test-and-punish-doesnt-educate-but-is-profitable-for-testing-companies

16. Wilson, J. (2013, June 25). Dumbing down America's teachers. *Education Week*, http://blogs.edweek.org/edweek/john_wilson_unleashed/2013/06/dumbing_down_americas_teachers.html

17. Weil, D. (2009). *Charter school movement: History, politics, policies, economics and effectiveness.* Amenia, NY: Grey House Publishing.

18. Ayers, B. (2012, November 8). Dear President Obama: Congratulations! *Good.is*, http://www.good.is/posts/an-open-letter-to-president-obama-from-bill-ayers

19. Ravitch, D. (2010). *The death and life of the great American school system: How testing and choice are undermining education.* New York: Perseus Books. [p. 171]

20. Holland, J., and Darling-Hammond, L. (2013, March 7). Teachers make handy scapegoats, but spiraling inequality is really what ails our education system. *AlterNet*, http://www.alternet.org/education/teachers-make-handy-scapegoats-spiraling-inequality-really-what-ails-our-education-system

21. Fabricant, M., and Fine, M. (2012). *Charter schools and the corporate makeover of public education: What's at stake?* New York: Teachers College Press. [p. 83]

22. Khadaroo, S. T. (2011, September 16). Wisconsin teachers retire in droves after union loss in bargaining fight. *Christian Science Monitor*, http://www.csmonitor.com/USA/Education/2011/0916/Wisconsin-teachers-retire-in-droves-after-union-loss-in-bargaining-fight

23. Wilson. Dumbing down America's teachers; Fitzhugh, C. (2013, June 26). State's treatment of teachers a recipe for disaster. *The Tennessean*, http://www.freenewspos.com/news/article/a/442177/today/state-39-s-treatment-of-teachers-is-a-recipe-for-disaster

24. Holland and Darling-Hammond. Teachers make handy scapegoats.

25. Berliner and Glass. *50 myths and lies that threaten America's public schools.* [p. 81]

Chapter Nine

Assumption 9

Alternative teacher licensure programs are better than traditional teacher education

THE ASSUMPTION

Those who would take down public schools are also seeking to do away with university-based teacher certification programs. The assumption here is that teacher preparation at colleges and universities is a waste of time. Alternative routes to licensure will attract higher-quality individuals into teaching and get them into the classroom faster.

Virtually every state now has alternative licensure programs that allow anyone with a college degree to start teaching with minimal preparation.[1] National programs like Teach for America (TFA) that place college graduates with no education background in classrooms with a few weeks of training are held up as models for what should be done. Privatized teacher licensure schemes are flourishing.

In many states, anyone who passes certain tests can be certified to teach, and online companies have been set up to prepare folks to pass the tests without ever having contact with a child or any experience in a classroom. The logic for dismantling the current teacher education system builds on the assumptions addressed above: teacher education schools are producing inept teachers and public schools are failing, so we need to rework both.

It is interesting to chart the evolvement of the concerted effort to discredit university-based teacher education. The same forces that are determined to do away with public education are aligned to attack traditional teacher preparation. They use the same tactics based on the same assumptions to achieve their ends.

Reformers argue that teacher education based in higher education institutions is failing and we have reports from conservative think tanks to prove it. The teacher education programs we currently have are loaded with unnecessary coursework, they have no standards about whom they let in and whom they graduate, and they are not preparing teachers who can increase the test scores of their future students.[2]

We need to make teacher educators accountable by getting rid of an inadequate accreditation system and by applying criteria established by outsiders who are not tied to the education establishment. Further, we need to assess teacher education programs by connecting their performance directly to the test scores of the teachers they produce. As with the bleak characterization of public schools, the reform discourse around teacher education programs portrays all schools of education as weak, out of date, and self-protective.

When programs at some of the top universities in the United States refuse to participate in an assessment organized by an outside agency with a clearly antagonistic agenda, they are chastised as having something to hide and threatened with being labeled as failures. When reports are pulled together comparing teachers from traditional preparation programs with alternatively licensed individuals (like those from TFA), data are selected that make it appear that the alternative licensure teachers are doing as well or better, while other data that show the weaknesses of the alternative programs are ignored.[3]

When university-based educators argue that learning *how* to teach is just as important as learning *what* to teach, they are dismissed as protecting their own turf. They are chastised for turning away well-educated individuals who want to teach but don't want to waste their time with all the "fluff" associated with earning a traditional teaching credential. It turns out not to matter how good traditional university-based programs are or how well their graduates teach; alternative licensure programs are assumed to be better.

DEBUNKING ASSUMPTION 9

Comprehensive, university-based teacher education programs are under attack, while alternative licensure schemes are expanding. In 2009, Secretary of Education Arne Duncan gave a speech entitled "Teacher Preparation: Reforming the Uncertain Profession."[4] Even though he has no preparation or experience himself as a teacher or teacher educator, he was ready to damn traditional university-based teacher preparation as mediocre at best. He didn't even have the charity to call it "an Uncertain Profession"; he went for the rhetorical coup de grace: "*the* Uncertain Profession." This signaled the beginnings of an effort on the part of educational reformers and their political allies to broaden their strategic offensive to include an attack on traditional teacher preparation.

The Department of Education assumes teacher educators are mediocre, so there is a push for more accountability in teacher preparation. As a result, states are being pressured to include the value-added scores of program graduates in determinations of program quality. Ignoring all the pitfalls associated with standardized testing and VAM, states have begun to use the average value-added test scores of the students of graduated teachers to assess teacher educator effectiveness.

Test and measurement experts point out the serious flaws in extending the already limited validity and reliability of VAM scores for estimating teachers' effectiveness to making guesses about the quality of teacher preparation programs those teachers attended. David Berliner and Gene Glass call using student test scores to judge the institutions that trained the teachers "foolishness squared."[5]

Specific issues include the following: VAMs provide a very limited view, leaving out several important dimensions of program quality; using average performance (as opposed to something like minimum level of performance of all graduates) may not be the most informative measure of program effectiveness; and nonrandom processes by which graduates are distributed across schools lead to biased estimates of program teachers' value-added scores.[6] Still, teacher preparation programs are now experiencing the same frustrations with unreliable VAM outcomes as their colleagues in public schools.

Not only do reformers paint teacher education programs as ineffective, they do their best to convince the public and our elected representatives that traditional programs create barriers that discourage individuals who are competent in their subject matter areas from becoming teachers. By the logic of reformers, successful teaching "is attributed to knowing what to teach versus ever learning how to teach, which makes 'traditional' teacher education not only irrelevant, but an unnecessary hurdle that keeps away the best and brightest."[7]

University-based teacher education is somehow insufficient for traditionally prepared teachers at the same time it is unnecessarily burdensome for those who already have training in a subject matter field or hold degrees (in anything but education) from elite universities. Ignoring the irony, reformers push for making traditional teacher education more accountable and rigorous at the same time they promote alternative routes that place "teachers" in classrooms with as little as four or five weeks of preparation.

The attack on university-based teacher education is exemplified by the rise in power and influence of the National Council on Teaching Quality (NCTQ), which discovered its niche within the reform agenda when it contracted with *US News and World Report* to assess schools of education across the nation. Coalitions of savvy administrators at some of the top research universities in the United States saw an ambush coming and refused to participate in NCTQ surveys designed to assess teacher education programs based on nonobjective evaluators' interpretations of catalog course descriptions and syllabi.

NCTQ's counter was to threaten to give failing grades to those who did not voluntarily provide data. When these threats did not produce capitulation, NCTQ collected whatever data they could from online sources and course materials pirated or purchased from students and others. NCTQ outcomes were predictable.

Universities and colleges, even those with well-documented successes and well-earned reputations as top-tier teacher education institutions, were given low marks and "consumer alerts" based on arbitrary criteria and distorted and incomplete data.[8] Still, NCTQ and other reform-bent enterprises continue to have the ear of the media, the public, and those who make policy regarding education and teacher preparation.

Alternative licensure approaches are widespread and take a variety of forms. Some states grant licenses to anyone who can pass certain tests, and online companies sell programs designed to prepare individuals to take those tests. Most states have set up or sanctioned fast-track preparation programs for teachers in high-need areas such as math, science, and special education.

Some school districts have proposed certifying teachers without applicants ever having any university-based preparation. Online universities are offering teacher education programs that require no face-to-face contact with instructors or students. Brick-and-mortar colleges and universities offer an array of alternative licensure programs, mostly in high-need areas and for second-career teachers.

Most visibly, programs like Teach for America (TFA) are placing newly graduated students from fields other than education in classrooms in underserved communities as an alternative to hiring fully prepared and licensed teachers. All of these programs, especially TFA (as described below), assume that learning *how to teach* is unimportant and, therefore, traditional teacher education is unnecessary.

University-based teacher preparation is not perfect, and efforts are underway to reshape the ways that programs are accredited, increase the entrance requirements for those wanting to become teachers, extend the amount of clinical practice required for licensure, and add performance-based indicators to assess the teaching abilities of prospective graduates.[9] But, those who want to destroy traditional teacher education do not acknowledge the strengths of university-based programs or that, like all professions, teacher educators are always trying to improve.

Radical reformers choose to ignore data that show that alternative routes to certification do not lead to improved student performance or teacher effectiveness.[10] They paint teacher education as a static, unitary entity, arguing that all teacher education institutions are terrible and unwilling to change.

Like teachers, teacher educators are trapped: damned if we do and damned if we don't. Damned if we add time to prepare teachers well; damned if we don't increase expectations for learning how to teach. Damned if we increase entrance requirements; damned if we don't let in anyone who already has expertise. Damned if we expect a full-year's internship experience for potential career teachers; damned if we don't find alternative fast tracks for those who want to teach for a while.

Teach for America symbolizes the assumption that teaching requires no special preparation; it hurts the schools and communities in which it operates; and it takes jobs away from real teachers. TFA was the brainchild of Wendy Koop, who created the organization based on her undergraduate thesis at Princeton University in 1989. Non-education university graduates (usually from elite universities) are recruited to teach in high-poverty schools. They commit to spending two years in the program and receive five weeks of summer training prior to being placed in classrooms.

TFA has become the darling of reform advocates. They love how easy it is to sell the idea that smart college grads who are committed to helping poor kids can take over classrooms with virtually no professional preparation. The same philanthropic entities that support reform in general give money to TFA, and the same forces that seek to privatize schooling via charters and alter legislation to diminish teacher professionalization are closely aligned with TFA.[11]

If your goal is to break what reformers see as higher education's monopoly on teacher preparation, TFA generates the perfect set of questions. If the best and the brightest college graduates are willing to teach for two years, why are traditional colleges of education not able to attract higher-caliber teacher candidates? If TFA recruits are willing to be placed in charter schools without any say in their working conditions, why should traditionally licensed teachers be any different? If TFA recruits with no professional training can raise test scores in hard-to-staff schools, why should others be forced to undergo the "mediocre" preparation provided by university-based teacher education programs?

As part of the radical reform network, TFA spends lots of money and resources on lobbying and public relations to be sure that questions like these get answered in ways that improve their economic and political positioning, while systematically devaluing traditionally prepared teachers and university-based teacher education. However, TFA's highly subsidized and widely publicized "successes" do not tell the whole story.

Critics have several concerns about TFA that reveal serious flaws beneath the glossy veneer of success. Some of these concerns include the following:

1. TFA is sold as a pathway to success in real professions. Critics have pointed out that fewer than 20 percent of TFA recruits are still teaching after five years, and most put in their two years and leave to pursue their real career interests in business, law, and other professions that are more lucrative and respected than teaching. The perception among many recruits is that service in TFA is a great résumé builder that will help them get into prestigious graduate programs, and this perception is fueled by TFA recruiters. [12]

2. TFA has been accused of showing preference for "Ivy League" graduates over signing up candidates who look like the students TFA assigns their recruits to teach. In its early years, TFA recruits came almost exclusively from elite private universities like Wendy Koop attended. Critics complain that the continuing spirit of attracting candidates from highly selective institutions leaves out graduates from colleges and universities that attract students with fewer monetary, academic, and social resources than those who attend elite schools. This greatly reduces the likelihood that poor and minority children will have TFA teachers who know and understand the impact of the contexts in which they live. [13]

3. TFA promotes a revolving-door conception of teaching that undermines the teaching profession and shortchanges the schools and communities in which recruits teach. Some cynics call TFA "Teach for Awhile." Research shows that all teachers are least effective during their first two years of teaching, so the majority of TFA recruits leave at about the time you would expect them to have a real impact. [14]

Conceptualizing teaching in poor urban and rural communities as a temporary service activity frames teaching as occupational activity that anyone can do and not important enough to train for or devote a career to. Worse, sending the least prepared teachers to temporarily occupy space in the schools with the highest needs cheats children, families, and communities at the bottom of the economic pyramid. [15]

4. TFA destroys the mentoring and relationship building provided by career teachers. All healthy organizations, including schools, have a mix of more- and less-experienced personnel. Effective schools need savvy, knowledgeable veterans to show the ropes to novice teachers. In the TFA model, inexperienced teachers are brought in to replace seasoned teachers or to take slots in charter schools that traditionally licensed teachers would not be hired to fill. [16] When everyone is a novice, who is capable of providing the support every professional needs to advance his or her career?

5. TFA "boot-camp" summer training reduces instruction to test preparation and classroom management to a set of tricks. Those who support TFA are the same reformers who measure school success strictly in terms of scores on standardized tests. It makes sense, then, that TFA recruits are given a crash course in how to increase test scores. What little time is left focuses on pre-

packaged classroom management advice that provides recruits with "cookie cutter" strategies for keeping students under control. [17]

Attention to alternative instructional approaches, nuanced understandings of student self-regulation, or explorations of the social realities that impact the educational opportunities of their students is missing from TFA summer training. In fact, former TFA recruits report that asking questions that call for a critical examination of what they are doing is discouraged by TFA staffers. [18]

> 6. TFA recruits don't recognize the negative impact they are having on schools, communities, or the teaching profession. Recruiting materials entice candidates by trumpeting TFA's mission of ending educational inequality. In reality, TFA does the opposite of its stated intent. It exacerbates one of the greatest inequalities in US education: low-income children of color are much more likely to be assigned to inexperienced and uncertified teachers. [19]

Students and parents in communities where TFA recruits are placed know the score. "Temps for African Americans" is another sardonic interpretation of the TFA acronym that rings true in communities that see their children being taught by "cultural tourists" who would never be allowed to teach in classrooms full of white middle-class students. [20] Further, TFA diminishes the professionalism of teachers. Teachers' professional status is undermined when teaching is viewed as something a person can do without formal preparation and when it is seen as a temporary job between college and a real career. [21]

> 7. TFA contracts with school systems and charter organizations to take jobs from experienced and newly licensed teachers. In the early years, TFA made its case for placing recruits in schools serving poor communities by claiming that there were teacher shortages in these areas. However, times have changed, and school districts are laying off teachers because of budget shortfalls.

TFA now asserts that although poor urban and rural schools may not be suffering an overall shortage of teachers, they are lacking the quality of teachers that TFA can provide. In fact, in places like Chicago, New York City, Philadelphia, Detroit, and New Orleans, thousands of teachers are being laid off at the same time districts have signed contracts with TFA stipulating that hundreds of untrained recruits will be hired each year. Even more galling, these contracts obligate districts to pay thousands of dollars in "finder fees" to the TFA organization for each recruit placed in their schools. [22]

As school budgets decline and TFA's "market share" increases, more veteran teachers will be laid off or forced out, and fewer traditionally trained new teachers will be able to find jobs. Of course, these are seen as victories in the eyes of education reform advocates. They see veteran educators as expensive deadwood and TFA recruits as archetype teachers of the future.

> 8. TFA self-reports of consistently positive outcomes have been questioned by those inside and outside the organization. Like other education reform entities, TFA stays in business because it is adept at creating and maintaining a certain image in the eyes of the public and public policy makers. They regularly bolster that image by producing and disseminating "data" that show the effectiveness of their programs.

TFA data have been called into question by independent research analysts, noting that issues with sample construction, matching procedures, and statistical analyses make it impossible to attribute outcomes reported in TFA studies to the impact of TFA teachers.[23] Also, former insiders with responsibility for TFA internal research have reported that statistics used to show significant gains for TFA teachers were unreliable and misleading.[24] Independent research comparing academic outcomes for students in TFA classrooms with those of other teachers is inconclusive.

Some studies show that new teachers from traditional teacher education programs do better, some show TFA teachers doing better with some students in some subjects, and other studies show no statistical difference between TFA and other new teachers.[25] These mixed results don't tell us much, but they certainly call into question the overwhelmingly positive outcomes pumped out by TFA itself.

> 9. TFA exemplifies the idea that extensive preparation is unnecessary for teaching success. In terms of negative consequences for our profession, the message that individuals with no specialized preparation can step into classrooms and teach effectively is the most damaging. TFA helped create and then benefitted immensely from the ethos of education reform that has swept this country.

Traditionally prepared teachers have been demonized, teacher professionalization has been trivialized, and teacher education has been marginalized. In the minds of those who would privatize public education and dramatically alter or do away with university-based teacher education, TFA is an unqualified success story. When stirred into the mix of reform elements critiqued in this book, TFA provides evidence that teaching is easy work that can be done by temporary workers without special preparation.

It is our responsibility as professional educators to debunk the assumptions of the reform advocates and challenge the assertions of TFA. One Chicago teacher eloquently illustrates the deficiencies of TFA in the following blog entry, in which she describes the differences between the preparation of traditionally trained teachers and the experience of TFA candidates, concluding with a keen insight into the relative effectiveness of each approach:

> Pre-service teachers are slowly introduced into teaching, beginning with hundreds of hours of observation in multiple settings, with much discussion, reflection, and study of pedagogy and child development along the way. We slowly step up our practice to individual tutoring, small group instruction, and short whole group lesson plans before moving on to student teaching placements for many months. This model of teacher prep minimizes the effect on children, and creates safe spaces for new teachers to practice under the watchful eye of a mentor. Compare that to TFA's model of novices taking turns teaching one single group of students for only four weeks then being placed in classrooms by themselves. Where is the time for observation and practice in many different settings/age groups/subject matters/ability levels? How can anyone even argue that the two types of training are comparable? And, if TFA truly offered higher-quality prep, why aren't schools serving upper-income students demanding first year TFA teachers? The idea of course is preposterous. Upper-income parents would never, ever, allow uncertified, unprepared novices to teach their own children. [26]

The same forces attacking public education are also targeting traditional teacher education. It's no coincidence that the super-wealthy individuals who bankroll efforts to reform public education also support those who want to dismantle traditional teacher education. It's not by chance that the politicians who rail against teachers also damn teacher educators. It's no fluke that the education entrepreneurs who are making a fortune setting up charter schools are in bed with those selling alternative licensure schemes like TFA.

It's not happenstance that those who are raking in millions from the test-based accountability systems that drive public schools are pushing to evaluate university-based teacher education programs based on the standardized test scores of students of program graduates. To think of the public school reform offensive as something separate from the attack on traditional teacher education is naive and dangerous for both those of us who work in K-12 and those of us preparing teachers in higher education.

The network of moneyed and political interests that drives education reform in general also provides support for the attack on traditional teacher education and the expansion of alternative routes to teacher credentialing. For example, the National Council on Teacher Quality (NCTQ), which has mounted a sustained a barrage of assaults on university-based teacher preparation, was founded by the conservative Thomas B. Fordham Foundation, receiving millions in grants from the George W. Bush Department of Education.

NCTQ helped create the American Board for the Certification of Teacher Excellence (ABCTE) and the computerized tests they use to grant teacher licensure online. They work hand in glove with philanthropies (e.g., those run by the Broad, Walton, and Gates families) that give vast amounts of money to pay for radical education reform initiatives, and they have close ties to organizations like Jeb Bush's Foundation for Excellence in Education (FEE), which makes no secret of its goal to corporatize public education.[27]

TFA provides another compelling example of the ways that reform initiatives that impact K-12 and higher education are networked. Like NCTQ, TFA receives funds from both private and public sources that stand squarely for market-based education reform across the board, including eight-figure annual support from the Gates, Walton, and Broad foundations.[28]

More troubling given their claim to want to improve the education of children living in neighborhoods characterized by poverty, TFA links with governmental, for-profit, and not-for-profit agencies that promote the charter school movement and set up charters that supplant public schools in communities with the most need.

It is estimated that as many as one-third of TFA recruits are placed in privately run charter schools.[29] As described above, TFA recruits are being placed in charter school jobs and public school classrooms ahead of experienced educators and new teachers trained in traditional programs, demonstrating that alternatively licensed teachers are just what's needed in the restructured education dream of reform advocates.

Teachers and teacher educators need to stand shoulder to shoulder to protect the teaching profession and public schooling in the United States. The connections among those who are leading the attack on teaching and public education are strong. The parts of those networks described in this section foreshadow a more complete exposé of how the powerful elements associated with education reform are aligned (see chapter 11).

No matter how daunting the task, our profession and the future of America's children depend on the willingness of all education professionals to band together and do all we can to combat attempts to degrade professionally trained teachers and discredit those who prepare them. Recognizing our common enemies gives us the solidarity we need to fight the good fight.

NOTES

1. Grossman, P., and Loeb, S. (Eds.). (2008). *Alternative routes to teaching: Mapping the new landscape of teacher education.* Cambridge, MA: Harvard University Press.

2. Zeichner, K., and Pena-Sandoval, C. (2015). Venture philanthropy and teacher education policy in the U.S.: The role of the New Schools Venture Fund. *Teachers College Record, 117*(6), http://www.tcrecord.org/Content.asp?ContentId=17539

3. Schneider, M. (2013, March 18). NCTQ's varicose reform. *Mercedes Schneider's Edu-Blog,* http://deutsch29.wordpress.com/2013/03/18/nctqs-varicose-reform

4. Duncan, A. (2009, October 22). Teacher preparation: Reforming the uncertain profession. Remarks at Teachers College, Columbia University, http://www.ed.gov/news/speeches/teacher-preparation-reforming-uncertain-profession

5. Berliner, D. C., and Glass, G. V. (2014). *50 myths and lies that threaten America's public schools: The real crisis in education.* New York: Teachers College Press. [p. 82]

6. Floden, R. E. (2012). Teacher value added as a measure of program quality: Interpret with caution. *Journal of Teacher Education, 63*(5), 356–360.

7. Kumashiro, K. K. (2012). *Bad teacher: How blaming teachers distorts the bigger picture.* New York: Teachers College Press. [p. 54]

8. For an example of a university response to NCTQ's evaluation, see Benner, S. (2013, June 29). Report doesn't reflect quality of UT programs that prepare teachers. *Knoxville News Sentinel,* http://www.knoxnews.com/news/2013/jun/29/susan-benner-report-UT-teacher-program/

9. American Association of Colleges of Teacher Education (2013). The changing teacher preparation profession. *Report from AACTE's Professional Education Data System,* http://aacte.org/news-room/announcements/aacte-releases-data-report-on-state-of-teacher-preparation.html

10. Grossman, and Loeb. *Alternative routes to teaching.*

11. Mayer, D. (2012, May 7). The ALEC—Stand for Children—Teach for America connection. *Great Schools for America,* http://www.greatschoolsforamerica.org/gsa-wp/the-alec-teach-for-america-connection/

12. Sommer, M. (2013, February 17). City schools to consider Teach for America program. *The Buffalo News,* http://www.buffalonews.com/20130227/city_schools_to_consider_teach_for_america_program.html

13. Naison, M. (2013, February 11). Why Teach for America isn't welcome in my class. *AlterNet,* http://www.alternet.org/education/why-teach-america-isnt-welcome-my-class

14. Ravitch, D. (2010). *The death and life of the great American school system: How testing and choice are undermining education.* New York: Perseus Books.

15. Naison, M. (2013, July 26). How TFA is destructive. *Diane Ravitch's Blog,* http://dianeravitch.net/2013/07/26/mark-naison-how-tfa-is-destructive

16. Naison. How TFA is destructive.

17. Naison. How TFA is destructive.

18. Singhal, N. (2012). Why I quit Teach for America to fight for public education. In N. Schniedewind and M. Sapon-Shevin (Eds.), *Educational courage: Resisting the ambush of public education* (pp. 65–71). Boston: Beacon Press.

19. Osgood, K. (2013, June 30). An open letter to new Teach for America recruits. *At the Chalk Face,* http://atthechalkface.com/2013/06/30/an-open-letter-to-new-teach-for-america-recruits

20. Hartman. Teach for America's hidden curriculum.

21. Milner, H. R. (2013, February 28). Policy reforms and the de-professionalization of teaching. National Education Policy Center, http://nepc.colorado.edu/publication/policy-reforms-deprofessionalization

22. Hartman. Teach for America's hidden curriculum; Osgood. An open letter to new Teach for America recruits.

23. Heilig, J. V., and Jez, S. J. (2010, June). Teach for America: A review of the evidence. Great Lakes Center for Education Research and Practice, http://www.greatlakescenter.org/docs/Policy_Briefs/Heilig_TeachForAmerica.pdf

24. Simon, S. (2012, August 16). Has Teach for America betrayed its mission? *Reuters,* http://www.reuters.com/article/2012/08/16/us-usa-education-teachforamerica-idUSBRE87F05O20120816.

25. For an overview of TFA research outcomes, see Ravitch, *The death and life of the great American school system.*

26. Osgood. An open letter to new Teach for America recruits.

27. Schneider. NCTQ's varicose reform.

28. Cersonsky, J. (2013, July 9). Teach for America's civil war. *The American Prospect,* http://prospect.org/article/teach-americas-civil-war

29. Simon. Has Teach for America betrayed its mission?

Chapter Ten

Assumption 10

Wealthy individuals, entrepreneurs, and politicians know more about education than school professionals

THE ASSUMPTION

It's hard to imagine another profession that would be placed in the position of being told what to do and how to do it by forces outside its ranks. One of the definitional characteristics of a profession is that it takes responsibility for maintaining its own integrity. Professions decide on the requirements for membership, establish criteria for acceptable practice, and develop means for applying sanctions when ethical expectations are not met.

Other professionals would never stand for attempts by wealthy individuals or politicians to impose alternate routes to certification and licensure. Can you imagine granting someone a license to practice medicine once he or she has had a few weeks training during the summer or passed on online exam?

No other professionals would allow outsiders to tell them how to do their work. Can you imagine telling architects exactly which principles they could utilize in their work, ensuring that common core designs were applied across the board?

Other professionals would not stand still if someone with no background in their field were put in charge of deciding the criteria for assessing their effectiveness. Can you imagine measuring the competence of a dentist based on how well his or her patients took care of their teeth? What's unthinkable for other professionals is taken for granted for teachers.

People who have amassed vast fortunes or have reached levels of importance in political life are pulling the strings in the effort to reform public education. No one challenges their right or capacity to make decisions that impact the lives of hundreds of thousands of professionals and millions of schoolchildren. What's worse is the dismissive attitude these powerful outsiders have about the expertise, experience, and knowledge of teachers, administrators, educational scholars, and other education professionals.

As the assumptions addressed above demonstrate, the rich and powerful folks behind current educational reform efforts think they know what the problems are and that it would be a waste of time to consult with those they believe to be a major source of those problems. Wealthy individuals and politicians know more about education than those who have made careers preparing for and practicing their profession.[1]

DEBUNKING ASSUMPTION 10

Educators' knowledge and experience are being trumped by reformers' gall and vast resources. Michael Edwards encapsulates what we are up against, with specific reference to Bill Gates:

> Gates is as big an influence on global health and education policy as any government, and the decisions he makes will affect the lives of millions. It's great that he and other philanthrocapitalists want to improve schools in America, but why should his ideas about how to accomplish that task win out over others just because he's rich?[2]

Why indeed? Those who bankroll the reform movement and who do their best to make or shape education policy (Bill Gates has been called the "Shadow Secretary of Education") are super-wealthy individuals who have no special preparation in education, have done no educational research, and have certainly never spent any time working as teachers.

In fact, almost everyone who is trying to dismantle public education never attended public schools at all; their privileged parents sent them to exclusive preschools, tony day schools, prestigious prep schools, and elite universities. They are happy to prescribe radical fixes for public schools, but it would be unthinkable to send their own children there.

Those of us who have committed our work lives to public education, who have devoted ourselves to understanding the complexities of the teaching/ learning process, who have honed our expertise in real public school contexts are not just ignored by those pulling the education reform strings, we are portrayed as an essential part of the problem. Reformers present themselves as caring about children, while teachers are painted as selfish and self-serving.[3]

Anyone who disagrees with the edicts of those in power is treated like a naughty child. Anyone who challenges the efficacy of the accountability movement is painted as anti-rigor. Anyone who raises questions about the market-based assumptions of the reform movement is labeled a socialist. Anyone who speaks up about the havoc reformers are wreaking on public schools is told, "I don't like your tone."

The timing has been perfect for venture philanthropists, corporate investors, conservative think tanks, and education entrepreneurs. School funding has been cut back, and the impression has been manufactured that public education needs dramatic change. Powerful individuals with enormous financial resources have stepped in and offered much-needed money to schools. [4]

But all that money has strings attached, and individuals with no special knowledge, expertise, or experience are having a sea-changing impact on education policy at the local, state, and national levels. In effect, being an outsider in the field of education turns out to be the first requirement for membership in this elite club. Teachers and other education professionals need not apply.

Educators' knowledge and experience are being trumped by reformers' connections and public relations savvy. Some commentators have likened the connections among the political, business, philanthropic, and entrepreneurial elites who run the education reform movement to membership at the "cool kids' table" in a high school cafeteria. [5] Everyone knows that a certain status must be attained to join the cool kids' table and that a certain set of norms must be adhered to in order to stay. At this cool kids' table, power and money are prerequisite for membership.

National and state political leaders from both parties qualify; scholars from conservative think tanks are welcome; philanthropic foundation executives are included; Wall Street hedge fund managers have a place; and entrepreneurs who have found ways to profit from setting up nonprofit education enterprises are at the table.

The norms that bind these cool kids together are familiar by now: more charters, more voucher programs, more testing for accountability, more rigorous evaluation of teachers, more closing of "failing" schools, more firing of "ineffective" teachers, more national standards/testing, more market-driven decision making, more pressure to do away with teachers' unions. [6]

Just like in high school, it would be unthinkable to allow any uncool people at the table, so teachers and others without power, money, or elite status have to sit somewhere else. Just like in high school, any consideration that there might be other ways to think about what it means to be cool never comes to mind. Professional educators, especially teachers, are seldom consulted and virtually never listened to as the reform agenda is rolled out.

Having a depth of knowledge about education is somehow seen as a limitation by reform advocates, while having a stockpile of practical experience in education is seen as an outright deficit. Teachers, teacher educators, education researchers, and teacher advocates who question the motives or tactics of the reform movers and shakers are labeled as obstructionists and worse, and their labels stick because of a willing fourth estate.

In an article in the *American Journalism Review*, Paul Farhi takes his fellow journalists to task for their inadequate and slanted coverage of the education reform movement in the United States. Using specific examples from print and broadcast media, Farhi makes a compelling case that journalists promote reformers' ideological positionings without looking beneath the surface of claims that schools are failing, teachers are to blame, and education is in crisis.[7]

Others have noted an "amiable conspiracy of silence" among the press, the academic community, and policy makers with regard to critiquing reform initiatives and exposing the interests of those who finance them.[8] An environment has been created in which it seems unthinkable for the press or anyone else to challenge the motives and tactics of the powerful interests that bankroll the education reform movement.

It seems clear that the influence and resources behind education reform have an impact on how it is covered in the media and approached by academics and politicians. Silence may indeed be golden if it means that superwealthy, super-powerful individuals might take offense if they are challenged. Reform advocates have the public relations savvy and connections to ensure that what the public sees and hears is on message, and the subtext of that message is always this: don't listen to educators.

Educators' knowledge and experience are being trumped by reformers' cooked data and deceptive exemplars. Yet another irony imbedded in reformers' assault tactics is their insistence that educators utilize data-based decision making and research-based practices at the same time reform advocates cherry-pick data to bolster their case and flatly ignore any research that shows the folly of their policies.

As documented above, reform advocates feed the news media headlines about the successes of charter schools, citing data that independent researchers have shown to be incomplete at best and misleading for sure. They trumpet the classroom accomplishments of alternatively prepared teachers, while their own testing experts confess that data were inadequate to support advocates' conclusions.

They promote merit pay strategies as ways to improve teacher outputs, ignoring studies that show pay-for-performance schemes do not work. They continue to insist that standardized testing and VAM assessment schemes are the coin of the realm for evaluating school performance, even though the reliability and validity of these measures has been called into question by top scholars and preeminent organizations in the field.

Further, the reformers' public relations machine has no qualms about highlighting programs and individuals as examples of what they are marketing, even when the spin needed to sell them is downright dizzying. As detailed earlier, massive efforts have been undertaken by radical reform advocates to close down community schools in urban areas and replace them with charter schools. These efforts include vilifying the public schools and their teachers and glorifying the charter alternatives.

It does not matter that the bases for making comparisons are rigged to pit the best-funded, most selective, most highly resourced charters against public schools that take all comers and starve for basic facilities, materials, and services. It does not matter that public schools overall do just as well as or outperform charter alternatives. It does not matter because in the logic of market-driven reform, the ends justify the means.

The heroes and heroines of the reform movement provide another example of the tactics reformers employ to promote their cause. It is fascinating that not one of the high-profile figures who symbolize education reform comes from the field of education. They may be experts at running giant corporations, starting nonprofits, getting elected to office, or securing appointments from their friends; but they are novices when it comes to educating children. Many have learned all they need to know to reshape American public education as Teach for America recruits.

Michelle Rhee is one such person, and her near-iconic status as a "radical" is emblematic of how effective reformers' efforts to extend their influence have been. Michelle Rhee has been featured in a popular movie, appeared on talk shows like *Oprah*, been the prime subject in several television documentaries, written her own books, and started her own education nonprofit. The reputation garnered from all these activities is based largely on her success as a TFA recruit in Baltimore inner-city schools and her subsequent tenure as Chancellor of District of Columbia Public Schools.

In DC, Rhee told principals and teachers to raise student test scores or lose their jobs; then she followed through on her threats by summarily firing principals and teachers and closing schools when scores did not improve. Even though her time was short in both Baltimore and Washington, Michelle Rhee has parlayed that time into a lucrative career as a high-profile education reformer.

The media and the public relations managers of education reform love her. It is never brought up that the miraculous gains claimed when she was doing her TFA time in Baltimore have been discredited. It never gets a mention that she was run out of DC after it was clear that her strong-arm tactics were creating widespread divisiveness and dissatisfaction while improving student performance only marginally, if at all.

It is treated as unimportant that charges of cheating, teaching to the test, and institutionalized fraud were the real outcomes of her time as DC Chancellor.[9] Michelle Rhee's story is the archetype version of the education reform story: if you tell it loud enough and often enough, it does not matter if the story is full of holes.

The well-developed knowledge base and hard-earned experience that educators bring to the table are no match for the distortions, deceptions, and hype that reformers use to get their way. After all, in the business model they want to apply to schooling, winning at any cost is the name of the game. Susan Ohanian and Marion Brady write:

> Future historians, trying to explain why Americans, at the turn of the 21st century, chose a path to education reform that made catastrophe all but inevitable, will have a difficult time unraveling the tangled weave of ideology, ignorance, hubris, secrecy, naïveté, greed, and unexamined assumptions that contributed to that catastrophe.[10]

Part I of this book has debunked many of the unexamined assumptions that are leading American education toward a catastrophic end. Part II will continue to unravel the snarl that threatens teachers and others who want to protect public education. The book will conclude by offering ways for education professionals, working alongside public school supporters, to confront those who would dismantle American schools as we know them.

NOTES

1. Edwards, M. (2010). *Small change: Why business won't save the world.* San Francisco: Berrett-Koehler.

2. Edwards. *Small change.* [p. 95]

3. Kuhn, J. (2014). *Fear and learning in America: Bad data, good teachers, and the attack on public education.* New York: Teachers College Press.

4. Kumashiro, K. K. (2012). *Bad teacher: How blaming teachers distorts the bigger picture.* New York: Teachers College Press.

5. Gabriel, T., and Medina, J. (2010, May). Charter schools' new cheerleaders: Financiers. *New York Times,* http://www.nytimes.com/2010/05/10/nyregion/10charter.html?page wanted=all percent_r=0

6. Horn, J., and Wilburn, D. (2013). *The mismeasure of education.* Charlotte, NC: Information Age Publishing; Gabriel and Medina. Charter schools' new cheerleaders.

7. Farhi, P. (2012, March 30). Flunking the test. *American Journalism Review,* http://www.ajr.org/article.asp?id=5280

8. Hess, F. H. (Ed.). (2005). *With the best on intentions: How philanthropy is reshaping K-12 education.* Cambridge, MA: Harvard Education Press. [p. 4]

9. Ravitch, D. (2011, March 29). Shame on Michelle Rhee: A new report shows student testing irregularities in D.C. under the leadership of reform advocate Michelle Rhee. *The Daily Beast,* http://www.thedailybeast.com/articles/2011/03/29/michelle-rhees-cheating-scandal-diane-ravitch-blasts-education-reform-star.html

10. Ohanian, S., and Brady, M. (2012, September 7). Outing ACT: Test-and-punish doesn't educate, but it's profitable for testing companies. *Truthout,* http://truth-out.org/news/item/11361-outing-act-test-and-punish-doesnt-educate-but-is-profitable-for-testing-companies [p. 1]

Part II

Speaking Truth to Power

The notion of "speaking truth to power" has its roots in the philosophical stance of the Religious Society of Friends (Quakers) in the eighteenth century. Over the years, Quakers have continued to practice this tenet as they seek alternatives to violence and war, and other individuals and groups have adopted this mantra as they have stood up to those who have much more power and influence.

Speaking truth to power is an ethical responsibility as much as a political strategy. As educators and others who want to stand up to the powerful forces bent on destroying public education, we have a moral obligation to give voice to the truth about reformers' ends and means. To remain silent and compliant when we know better is the ethical equivalent of capitulation and complicity.

As a political strategy, speaking truth to power provides a means for bringing pressure on forces that are used to having things their own way. As is made clear in chapter 11, those running the education reform show have so much wealth and power that their influence is virtually never challenged. Telling the truth every chance we get and in every forum we can find can have an impact on how reformers' demagoguery is perceived and how future education policy is enacted.

The three chapters in Part II provide information about who has the power and how they use it, alternative narratives to counter the stories of crisis told by education reformers, and strategies for reclaiming the teaching profession. Chapter 11 details how the big three education philanthropies (Gates, Walton, and Broad), along with the American Legislative Exchange Council

(ALEC) and Pearson Education, scaffold the complex web of forces promoting the reform agenda.

Chapter 12 presents a set of alternative stories based on four meaningful purposes for public education. These stories provide counters to the grand narrative of school failure and teacher incompetence that reform advocates have told so many times that its fidelity is taken for granted. The narratives give educational professionals, parents, students, and other public education supporters something to say when they stand up to those in power.

Chapter 13 builds on the rest of this book, offering specific strategies for resisting the privatization of public education and challenging the demonization of teachers. As strategies are described, specific examples of how educators have enacted them are presented. In addition, references and an appendix are provided to take readers to resources they can use to bolster their efforts to speak truth to power.

Chapter Eleven

Exposing the Forces Behind Educational Reform

Paranoiacs worry that amorphous entities are threatening them, as in, "*They* are out to get me!" Teachers are not paranoid. We know we are the current targets of opportunity, and we have clear evidence of who is out to get us. This chapter exposes some of the most influential and pervasive forces driving market-based reform efforts. It names who *They* are and explores the complex network of connections among the individuals and entities aligned to demean our profession and reconfigure education in America.

In the first section of this chapter, an overview of the money and influence that drive educational reform is presented. Then, the scope and depth of influence of "the big three" (Gates, Walton, and Broad) are explored. Following that, sections detailing the involvement of the American Legislative Exchange Council (ALEC) and the Pearson Education Corporation are laid out. As will be evident below, when you follow the money, you find that Gates, Walton, Broad, ALEC, and Pearson link directly or indirectly to each other and to virtually all of the players in the educational reform game.

FOLLOW THE MONEY

In chapter 7, a description and critique of what Michael Edwards identified as "philanthrocapitalism" was presented.[1] This general shift from philanthropic *giving* to strategic *investing* certainly fits the world of education reform. Rather than looking for opportunities to support organizations doing good things, as traditional philanthropies have done, philanthrocapitalists (also called venture philanthropists) have specific goals and strategies in mind, and they invest their money where they think their return will be maximized.

A 2014 study of how philanthropy has expanded its role in the education policy arena shows education foundations are increasingly politically engaged. Unlike the past, current foundations support groups involved in policy advocacy, "including organizations that promote competition with public sector institutions."[2] Philanthrocapitalists understand that supporting challengers to traditional school policy advances their own aims.

Joining with corporations with vested interests, venture capitalists, hedge-fund managers, and local philanthropists, giant venture philanthropies provide reform money with strings. Their ideological agenda is based on neoliberal economic tenets: privatization, efficiency, deregulation, competition, and anti-unionism.[3] Schools or organizations with different values need not apply.

The strategic initiatives that those who bankroll reform expect are familiar. They include: charter schools, voucher schemes, school choice, accountability based on test scores, teacher evaluation based on test scores, data-driven decision making, elimination of teacher tenure, differential pay for teachers (not based on education or experience), alternative certification for teachers and school leaders, teacher education evaluation based on test scores, nationalized curriculum and testing, sanctions for low-performing teachers and schools, rewards for high-performing schools and teachers, and destabilization of teachers' unions.[4]

The amounts of money involved in supporting the reform agenda are staggering. The Gates Foundation alone poured an estimated $3.4 billion into educational reform initiatives between 1999 and 2014.[5] But the potential returns on these investments are astonishing too. Estimates in the $600 billion per year range are common projections of the market share for educational entrepreneurs.[6]

This leads investment managers to proclaim to potential clients that "an entire ecosystem of investment opportunity" is opening up[7] and a *Forbes* magazine pundit to announce, "I want all entrepreneurs to take notice that [public education] is a multi-hundred billion dollar opportunity."[8] There is big money to be made from the privatization of schools.

The Gates, Broad, and Walton fortunes are the sources for most of the philanthropic investment in educational reform, and the extent of their reach will be detailed below, but they are not alone. Other prominent philanthropies that are heavily invested include the Michael and Susan Dell Foundation, the Donald and Doris Fisher Fund, the Lynde and Harry Bradley Foundation, the Richard and Helen DeVos Foundation, and the Charles Koch Foundation.[9]

Foundations such as those named fund other venture philanthropies that specifically target radical education reform, such as the Charter Schools

Growth Fund and the NewSchools Venture Fund. [10] What is more, the mostly nonprofit organizations set up to attract venture philanthropists' dollars almost always include representatives of the sending organizations on their boards of directors. In fact, looking at who sits on the boards of the major private, nonprofit, governmental and quasi-governmental entities involved in education reform, it is easy to see the close linkages among the parties involved. [11]

One example of the intricate interconnections among parties with a vested interest in education reform is Jeb Bush's Foundation for Excellence in Education (FEE). E-mails have established that FEE has worked with ALEC and public officials across the country to write education laws that directly benefit the corporations that fund FEE and advance the radical reform agenda. The "experts" that serve as members or staff of these entities are part of an interdependent network of right-wing groups that spend their time writing legislation, lobbying, and peddling influence. [12]

Further, FEE pays the way for legislators and education officials to attend education reform summits, where time is set aside for donors to meet with "Chiefs for Change," a FEE-sponsored group of current and former state chief school officers. The donors supporting these summits include familiar foundations and business interests, including the Walton Foundation, Microsoft, McGraw-Hill Education, the Pearson Foundation, K12, and Charter Schools USA. [13] The purposes of connections like those defining how FEE operates are unmistakable and will be further illuminated in the discussion of the big three below.

Another dimension of the cross-pollination that characterizes groups pushing for education reform is the network of think tanks funded by foundations and corporate interests. Examples include the American Enterprise Institute, the Fordham Institute, the Heritage Foundation, the Hoover Institute, and the Policy Innovators in Education Network. Representatives from these think tanks work collaboratively with each other and other reform agents to put on conferences and prepare publications that advance their shared interests. [14]

The complexity of interconnectedness is rivaled only by the extent of influence of these reform groups. During the first decade of the twenty-first century, when the US economy was in dire straits and state and school district budgets were being slashed, reform advocates took the opportunity to offer money when it was most needed—but at a price. Reformers' impact multiplied in direct proportion to their investments, and their influence "set the policy agenda not only for school districts, but also for states and even the U.S. Department of Education." [15]

THE BIG THREE

The discussion to follow reveals the extent to which the big three philanthropies have been exerting their influence on the education reform movement. The interrelationships described are summarized in figure 11.1, which maps the connections among the philanthropic investments of the Gates, Walton, and Broad foundations.[16] The figure shows initiatives that are funded by all three foundations and breaks out those supported by two and those funded by one of these major foundations.

All three foundations invest in more enterprises than are identified in the graphic, but those included are significant exemplars of where the money goes. The education entities listed have been identified using tax records, foundation reports, and other reliable sources.[17] In figure 11.1, funding recipients are listed in alphabetical order within donor groups, but the description to follow combines recipients in like categories within the donor groupings.

The big three all invest heavily in charter school initiatives. The ones in which they are jointly invested include Achievement First (charter schools in Connecticut, New York, and Rhode Island), Aspire Public Schools (a charter management organization with schools in California and Tennessee), California Charter Schools Association (member organization supporting 1,130 California charter schools), KIPP (charter schools in twenty states and the District of Columbia),[18] the National Alliance for Public Charter Schools (the leading national nonprofit promoting the charter school movement), and the NewSchools Venture Fund (nonprofit venture philanthropy firm aiming to accelerate charter school growth).[19]

All three support Education Pioneers and Teach for America (TFA). Both of these organizations target college students who are not specifically trained to be teachers or school leaders. TFA places graduates with bachelor's degrees in hard-to-staff schools. Education Pioneers recruits, trains, and places graduate students from disciplines other than education in summer positions in urban school districts, education reform nonprofits, and charter management organizations across the country.

The big three mutually invest in Education Reform Now (ERN), Jeb Bush's Foundation for Educational Excellence (FEE),[20] and Parent Revolution.[21] ERN promotes national and state education reform, advocates for educational change, and educates policy makers on reform issues. FEE (described above) promotes a reform agenda that includes school choice, outcome-based funding, ending teacher tenure, and grading schools on an A–F basis. Parent Revolution advocates for parent trigger laws, providing training and support for those seeking to enact or take advantage of such laws.

In addition, each of the big three has contributed significant moneys to the National Council for Teacher Quality (NCTQ) and the National Governors Association (NGA). NCTQ began as a reform-focused think tank and has

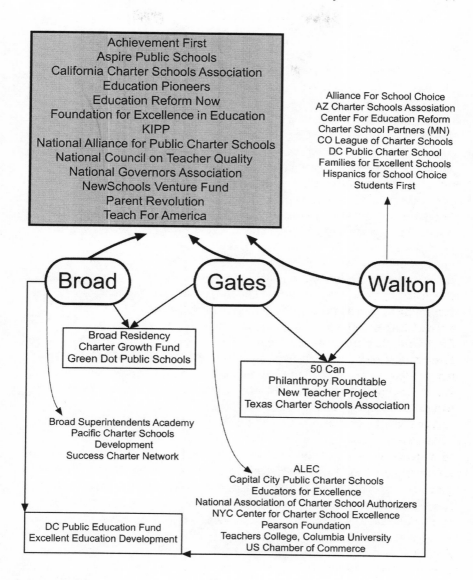

Figure 11.1.

become best known for the evaluation and ranking of teacher education programs it undertakes each year and publishes in *US News and World Report*. The NGA is one of the prime movers behind the Common Core State Standards initiative, and much of the money invested by the big three has gone toward creating and promoting the Common Core.

As noted above, education reform movers and shakers share a commitment to neoliberal ideologies and market-based strategies, and as is evident in where they put their money, the big three are no exception. The same kinds of investments characterize the giving when two of the big three are involved.

Continuing the pattern of funding organizations that champion charter schools, both the Gates and Broad foundations fund Green Dot Public Schools (one of the three largest charter school operators in the nation) and the Charter Growth Fund (a nonprofit that invests capital to expand the impact of the nation's highest-performing charter operators). Walton and Broad fund Excellent Education Development (supplying business and support services for California's high-achieving charter schools), while Gates and Walton both fund the Texas Charter School Association (representing more than 90 percent of charter schools in Texas—over 550 schools).

In addition, the Gates and Walton foundations both invest in 50 Can (a think tank and advocacy organization that promotes state-level education reform), the Philanthropy Roundtable (an organization of organizations that assists donors in achieving their philanthropic intent), and the New Teacher Project (nonprofit started by Michelle Rhee that established alternative routes to certification for teachers in high-needs schools).

Both Walton and Broad finance the D.C. Public Education Fund (a nonprofit that negotiated a contract that allowed the DC school district to reward teachers for performance and not seniority).[22] And the Gates Foundation has contributed millions to Broad Residency (a Broad-sponsored program that places individuals from outside education in full-time managerial positions in school districts, charter school organizations, and state and federal education departments).[23]

In addition to organizations funded with Gates and/or Walton, the Eli and Edythe Broad Foundation independently invests in charter initiatives such as Pacific Charter Schools Development (marshals resources to secure adequate space for charter schools in urban settings) and Success Charter School Network (formerly Harlem Success Academy–operates twenty-two charter schools in New York City). Broad also finances the Broad Superintendents Academy, which provides training to prepare superintendents to pioneer breakthrough initiatives to reform public education.

The Walton Family Foundation has school choice as a target initiative. It provides financial support to the Alliance for School Choice, which provides policy and program expertise as well as strategies and guidance for implementing and defending school choice programs. The Hispanics for School Choice initiative in Wisconsin is also supported. In addition, Walton funds the Center for Education Reform, which works with legislators and policy makers across the states to write and pass laws that increase school choice opportunities.

The Walton Family Foundation is also heavily invested in the charter school movement. It funds state charter school organizations in Arizona, Minnesota, Colorado, and the District of Columbia. The foundation also provides support to Families for Excellent Schools, which advances policy and political changes in support of charter schools. And Walton supports Michelle Rhee's Students First initiative, set up to build a national movement to pursue transformative school reform.

The Bill and Melinda Gates Foundation invests in several educational reform entities beyond those they share with Broad and Walton. These include charter-focused organizations such as Capital City Public Charter School (first parent-started District of Columbia charter school), the National Association of Charter School Authorizers (provides expertise, assistance, and guidance to agencies responsible for authorizing charter schools), and the New York City Center for Charter School Excellence (stimulates and supplies charter schools in NYC).

Gates also funds Educators for Excellence, a nonprofit started by Teach for America alumni with the aim of instituting merit pay approaches and ending seniority as a metric for teacher pay and continued employment.[24] The Gates Foundation has awarded several grants to Teachers College, Columbia University, to support efforts that include improving journalistic coverage of education reform initiatives. In the past, Gates has contributed to ALEC to support education reform efforts,[25] but the foundation distanced itself when ALEC came under fire for its support of voter identification laws and its part in crafting "stand your ground" legislation that came to light during the Trayvon Martin case.[26]

The Gates Foundation has invested massive moneys to develop, promote, and defend the Common Core State Standards (CCSS).[27] Examples of where the money has gone include partnering with the Pearson Foundation to create a digital learning system designed to teach K-12 math and language arts Common Core Standards[28] and funding efforts by the US Chamber of Commerce to rally state and local chapters to fight off resistance to CCSS.[29]

The big three, along with an array of smaller venture philanthropies, have placed their unmistakable stamp on the education reform movement. Walton, Broad, and Gates are anchors in a complex and powerful network of money and influence that are having an astounding impact on the lives of students, schools, and communities. Identifying who is out to get teachers gives us knowledge we can use to resist. The workings of ALEC and Pearson and their own outsized influence on education reform are taken up next.

ALEC

The American Legislative Exchange Council is an organization of approximately two thousand conservative state legislators. Its primary function is the production of template-based legislative initiatives that promote neoliberal, market-based approaches in many public spheres, including education, health care, the environment, the economy, voting laws, and public safety.

ALEC's mode of operation is to send prewritten bills to state legislators, who fill in the blank where it says "State of _____." The legislators put their names on the bills and throw them in the hopper for legislative action. Formed in 1973, ALEC works behind the scenes to influence policy across the board; but their activities have been criticized and they have lost some of their philanthropic and corporate donors as some of their tactics and far-right political orientation have been exposed.[30]

ALEC continues to be well funded, with over three hundred corporate sponsors, and their impact continues to be immense, especially in the arena of education reform legislation at the state level. In the first six months of 2013 alone, at least 139 bills or state budget provisions with ALEC's education reform stamp on them were introduced in forty-three states and the District of Columbia. Among these were initiatives to:

- create or expand taxpayer-funded voucher programs;
- provide tuition tax credits to parents sending their children to private schools, including religious institutions;
- use tax dollars to fund the tuition of students attending virtual schools run by private online providers;
- offer teaching credentials to individuals with subject-matter expertise but no background in education;
- require educators to "teach the controversy" when it comes to climate change;
- create opportunities to privatize public schools or fire principals and teachers via "parent trigger" legislation; and
- take away local school boards' responsibility for authorizing charter schools and turn it over to appointed, state-level authorizing bodies.[31]

ALEC is relentless, well organized, and well funded. When ALEC templates are tabled in committee or defeated on the floor, they are tweaked (or not) and resubmitted next legislative session. ALEC keeps tabs on legislative activity and organizes conferences, during which legislators and business leaders work together to shape future policy.

ALEC's financial support comes from large corporations like State Farm Insurance, Intel, and Microsoft. They also receive moneys from corporations that have a direct financial interest in education reform legislation, including

K12 (the largest provider of virtual schooling) and Connections Academy (now owned by Pearson Education, which sells online lessons to charter schools and school districts).[32]

ALEC also has many cross-connections with other education reform entities, including Jeb Bush's Foundation for Excellence in Education (FEE), an organization funded by the big three. ALEC and FEE share "experts" as members or staff. They collaborate on the annual ALEC "report card," which assesses states based on their allegiance to ALEC's policy agenda.[33] One critic argued that grading this way was tantamount to a teacher assessing you not on how well you understood the material, but rather on "to what extent you agreed with your teacher's strange policy positions."[34]

It should be no surprise that states whose education leaders are tied into FEE's Chiefs for Change and whose legislators are actively promoting ALEC's policy agenda score highest on this so-called report card. Paralleling similar assessments such as those imposed on teacher preparation programs by the National Council on Teacher Quality (also funded by the big three), grades are based on criteria that measure compliance with the arbitrary standards of the assessing organization.

It is hard to underestimate the impact of ALEC on the education reform movement. Diane Ravitch names ALEC as the driving force behind state-level efforts to privatize public education.[35] Along with the big three and Pearson Education, ALEC certainly counts as an important segment of the "they" who are out to get teachers and do away with public school education as we know it. Appendix A is a sample list of education reform legislation proposed by ALEC, including brief summaries of bills and links to the ALEC website for further illumination.

PEARSON

Pearson Education proclaims itself the "world's leading education business." Based in England, Pearson began as a small building firm in 1844. In the 1950s, it expanded its holdings into the publishing business with the purchase of the *Financial Times*. From the 1960s on, it merged with or purchased a series of competing publishing houses. With the acquisition of Simon and Schuster Education in 1998, Pearson Education was born.[36] According to its website,

> Pearson Education leads in every major sector of educational publishing, both in the US and internationally. Over 100 education brands including Scott Foresman, Prentice Hall, Allyn and Bacon, Addison-Wesley, Silver, Burdette and Ginn, Longman, Benjamin Cummings and Macmillan Publishing USA fall under Pearson's umbrella.

This multinational corporation with annual sales in the billions did not stop after taking over the educational publishing industry. Pearson Learning has continued to grow, expanding its reach into educational testing, curriculum development, cyber schooling, online course delivery, charter schools, teacher evaluation, and more. Its impact on US schooling has been magnified by Pearson's strategic positioning as a business that is ready to supply the needs created by the educational reform movement.

In fact, critics argue that Pearson's business model is to influence the politically based process that makes the rules on which educational reform is based, then match their own products to the rules they helped define.[37] They accuse Pearson (and the Pearson Foundation) of blurring the lines among for-profit, nonprofit, and government systems to advance their own bottom line.[38] Some key examples of activities and enterprises that connect Pearson to the reform of education in the United States are presented below.

The Common Core State Standards. Pearson has a history of partnerships with the National Governors Association and the Council of Chief State School Officers. These are the two groups on the nameplate of the Common Core State Standards (CCSS). This is a place where the boundary between Pearson the company and Pearson the foundation becomes blurry. The Pearson Foundation promotes the common core, while (as is evident below) Pearson the corporation markets materials to make CCSS happen in the states and schools.[39]

enVisionMATH Common Core. Pearson even included "Common Core" as part of the name of this comprehensive K-6 mathematics curriculum. Their website touts that *"enVisionMATH Common Core* was built from the ground up to meet the Common Core State Standards" and will enable educators to "teach all of the Standards for Mathematical Content." The components of the program include hard and digital versions of texts, teachers' editions, workbooks, and myriad other materials.[40]

Digital Instructional Resources. In an April 2011 press release, the Pearson Foundation announced a partnership with the Bill and Melinda Gates Foundation to create a full series of digital instructional resources to teach the CCSS. Online K-12 courses in math and reading/English language arts "will enable teachers and students to access the latest and most effective digital learning technologies as they prepare to meet the internationally benchmarked college readiness goals of the Common Core Standards."[41]

Smarter Balanced and PARCC Assessments. The Smarter Balanced Assessment Consortium and the Partnership for Assessment of Readiness for College and Careers (PARCC) both received grants from the federal Race to the Top Assessment Program to create systems to assess CCSS. They jointly hired Pearson to develop a "Technology Readiness Tool" to assess states' capacities to administer the new digitally based assessments.[42] In addition,

Pearson and the Educational Testing Service have contracts with nineteen PARCC states to develop PARCC test items. [43]

edTPA. In addition to its many ties with the CCSS, Pearson is also involved in reform efforts aimed at teacher preparation and licensure. Pearson is contracted to deliver edTPA (formerly Teacher Performance Assessment) in more than twenty-five states. This online performance-based assessment developed by Stanford University (with support from Pearson) requires student registration, account management, portfolio submissions, scoring, and results reporting—all provided by Pearson. Critics worry that Pearson is essentially taking over teacher certification for their states to meet "reform" expectations build into Race to the Top applications. [44]

Connections Academy. FEE, ALEC, and other education reform agents have made a concerted effort to legislate public funding for cyber charter schools. [45] In 2011, Pearson entered the virtual charter schools market with the acquisition of Connections Education (behind K 12, the second-largest provider of cyber charters). It is worth noting that Mickey Revenaugh, who cofounded Connections Education, was also cochair of the ALEC Education Task Force that drafted legislation authorizing virtual charters. [46] Connections Academy is indeed connected.

Charter Schools. Marketing services and materials to charter schools, the conglomerate announces on its website, "Pearson shares your vision." Pearson's materials include textbooks that are available in multiple formats, as well as multimedia assets, educational software, test preparation materials, resources for teacher training and development, and materials for parents. Their website invites potential customers to "[l]earn how your charter school can partner with Pearson to create solutions that complement your mission." [47]

The examples above show that Pearson has worked hard to position itself to complement the mission of contemporary education reform. Even though they are a British company, their influence on education in the United States is ubiquitous. They are savvy to how neoliberal approaches to education reform work, and they are at the ready with the market-based solutions such approaches require.

Abby Rapoport offers an example of the long reach of Pearson in the state of Texas:

> Pearson, one of the giants of the for-profit industry that looms over public education, produces just about every product a student, teacher or school administrator in Texas might need. From textbooks to data management, professional development programs to testing systems, Pearson has it all—and all of it has a price. For statewide testing in Texas alone, the company holds a five-year contract worth nearly 500 million dollars to create and administer exams. If students should fail those tests, Pearson offers a series of remedial-learning products to help them pass. Meanwhile, kids are likely to use textbooks from

Pearson-owned publishing houses like Prentice Hall and Pearson Longman. Students who want to take virtual classes may well find themselves in a course subcontracted to Pearson. And if the student drops out, Pearson partners with the American Council on Education to offer the GED exam for a profit. [48]

Pearson is a business with one motive: maximum profit. The company and its foundation have been hugely successful in helping to set the reform agenda and then supplying the elements needed to implement it. It is reasonable for all those who care about public education to ask: "Are these the people we want designing tests, lessons, and curriculum for our students and deciding who is qualified to be a teacher?"[49]

The network of forces working to privatize public education in the United States is formidable. The players in the education reform game are wise to the political realities that undergird policy making, they are aware of the public relations strategies needed to sway popular opinion, and they are shrewd investors who know how to make their money work for them. Gates, Walton, Broad, ALEC, and Pearson are masters at manipulating the game in their favor; but as has been shown, they are not alone.

The premise for the title of one of Amy Tan's novels comes from an allegory that fits the logic of those who stand to profit from radical education reform. In the allegory, a fisherman gets rich by claiming that he is "saving fish from drowning" (Tan's title). He nets the fish and places them on the bank where they flop and twirl until they lie still. He announces that he did his best but is once again too late to save them and takes the fish to market to fetch a fine price. [50]

The powerful interests that want to reform schooling use a parallel line of flimflam. They claim to be saving public education from itself. They create an imaginary crisis for which they have magic solutions. When those solutions fail, they claim to have done their best, then go off to count the massive amounts of money they have netted from their disingenuous efforts.

As has been established in Part I of this book, public schools do not need to be saved from drowning. The fake promises hawked by entities that stand to profit from appearing to "save" American education can and must be challenged. The next two chapters describe ways to talk back to those in power and suggest strategies for reclaiming the teaching profession.

NOTES

1. Edwards, M. (2010). *Small change: Why business won't save the world.* San Francisco: Berrett-Koehler.

2. Reckhow, S., and Snyder, J. W. (2014). The expanding role of philanthropy in education politics. *Educational Researcher*, 43(4), 186–195. [p. 193]

3. Kumashiro, K. K. (2012). *Bad teacher: How blaming teachers distorts the bigger picture.* New York: Teachers College Press.

4. Schniedewind, N. (2012). A short history of the ambush of public education. In N. Schniedewind and M. Sapon-Shevin (Eds.), *Educational courage: Resisting the ambush of public education* (pp. 4–22). Boston: Beacon Press; Kumashiro. *Bad teacher.*

5. Layton, L. (2014, June 7). How Bill Gates pulled off the swift Common Core revolution. *The Washington Post*, http://www.washingtonpost.com/politics/how-bill-gates-pulled-off-the-swift-common-core-revolution/2014/06/07/a830e32e-ec34-11e3-9f5c-9075d5508f0a_story.html

6. Horn, J., and Wilburn, D. (2013). *The mismeasure of education.* Charlotte, NC: Information Age Publishing.

7. Simon, S. (2012, August 2). Private firms seeking profits from U.S. public schools. *Reuters*, http://in.reuters.com/article/2012/08/02/usa-education-investment-idINL2E8J15FR20120802[p. 1]

8. Naveen, J. (2013, March 24). Rethinking education: Why our education system is ripe for disruption. *Forbes*, http://www.forbes.com/sites/naveenjain/2013/03/24/disrupting-education/[p. 1]

9. Kumashiro. *Bad teacher.*

10. Kumashiro. *Bad teacher.*

11. Fabricant, M., and Fine, M. (2012). *Charter schools and the corporate makeover of public education: What's at stake?* New York: Teachers College Press.

12. Strauss, V. (2013, January 30). E-mails link Bush's foundation, corporations and education officials. *Washington Post*, http://www.washingtonpost.com/blogs/answer-sheet/wp/2013/01/30/e-mails-link-bush-foundation-corporations-and-education-officials/

13. Horn, J. (2013, February 1). How Jeb Bush''s FEE became the conduit for corporate cash to make ed policy. *Schools Matter*, http://www.schoolsmatter.info/2013/02/how-jeb-bush-fee-became-conduit-for.html

14. Ravitch, D. (2013). *Reign of error: The hoax of the privatization movement and the danger to America's public schools.* New York: Alfred A. Knopf.

15. Ravitch, D. (2010). *The death and life of the great American school system: How testing and choice are undermining education.* New York: Perseus Books. [p. 200]

16. Jessica Stone was instrumental in creating the graphic for figure 11.1 and for tracking down the information summarized there. She also collected and organized the information included in appendices A and B.

17. Data on Gates Foundation investing were drawn from the Foundation's 990-PF tax statement for 2012, http://www.gatesfoundation.org/~/media/GFO/Who%20We%20Are/Financials/2012%20BMGFT%20990PF%20PUBLIC%20DISCLOSURE%20FINAL.pdf. Information about giving for the other foundations was taken from each organization's 2013 financial report: (a) Broad http://www.broadeducation.org/investments/current_investments/investments_all.html; (b) Walton http://www.waltonfamilyfoundation.org/about/2013-grant-report. Other sources and websites utilized are cited separately below.

18. Ravitch. *Reign of error.*

19. NewSchools Venture Fund website, http://www.newschools.org/donors

20. Foundation for Excellence in Education website, http://excelined.org/about-us/meet-our-donors/

21. Parent Revolution website, http://parentrevolution.org/our-funders/

22. Walton Family Foundation website, http://www.waltonfamilyfoundation.org/mediacenter/top-five-grantees

23. Barkan, J. (2013, Winter). Got dough? How billionaires rule our schools. *Dissent*, http://www.dissentmagazine.org/article/got-dough-how-billionaires-rule-our-schools

24. Pelto, J. (2014, May 23). Teacher-led organization that gives teachers a meaningful voice in policy is expanding in CT! *Wait What?*, http://jonathanpelto.com/tag/educators-4-excellence/

25. Gates Foundation website, http://www.gatesfoundation.org/How-We-Work/Quick-Links/Grants-Database/Grants/2011/11/OPP1044898

26. Lorbor, J. (2012, April 9). Gates foundation will no longer make grants to ALEC nonprofit. *Roll Call*, http://www.rollcall.com/news/gates_foundation_will_withdraw_support_for_alec_nonprofit-213689-1.html

27. Layton. How Bill Gates pulled off the swift Common Core revolution.

28. Pearson Education website, http://www.pearsoned.com/pearson-foundation-partners-bill-melinda-gates-foundation-create-digital-learning-programs/#.U9o79ijEcQJ

29. Molnar, M. (2014, January 28). State Chambers of Commerce defend Common Core. *Education Week*, http://www.edweek.org/ew/articles/2014/01/29/19chambers_ep.h33.html

30. Ravitch, D. (2012, May 1). What you need to know about ALEC. *Bridging Differences*, http://blogs.edweek.org/edweek/Bridging-Differences/2012/05/dear_deborah_since_the_2010.html

31. Fischer, B. (2013, July 16). Cashing in on kids: 139 ALEC bills in 2013 promote private, for-profit education model. *PR Watch*, http://www.prwatch.org/news/2013/07/12175/cashing-kids-139-alec-bills-2013-promote-private-profit-education-model

32. Graves, L. (2012, November 28). Taxpayer enriched companies back Jeb Bush's Foundation for Excellence in Education, its buddy ALEC, and their "reforms." *PR Watch*, http://www.prwatch.org/news/2012/11/11883/taxpayer-enriched-companies-back-jeb-bushs-foundation-excellence-education-its-bu

33. Graves. Taxpayer enriched companies back Jeb Bush's Foundation for Excellence in Education, its buddy ALEC, and their "reforms."

34. Beilke, D. (2012, February 2). ALEC education "academy" launches on island resort. *PR Watch*, http://www.prwatch.org/news/2012/02/11272/alec-education-academy-launches-island-resort[p. 1]

35. Ravitch. What you need to know about ALEC.

36. Pearson website, http://timeline.pearson.com/

37. Pegwpen. (2012, April 29). Pearson, ALEC, and the brave new (corporate) world: Stand up to Pearson now! *United Opt Out*, http://unitedoptout.com/2012/04/27/boycott-pearson-now/

38. Job, J. (2012, November). The Pearson monopoly. *NewTeacher*, http://teacherblog.typepad.com/newteacher/2012/11/on-the-rise-of-pearson-oh-and-following-the-money.html

39. Singer, A. (2012, June 8). Hacking away at the Pearson octopus. *Huffington Post*, http://www.huffingtonpost.com/alan-singer/hacking-away-at-the-pears_b_1464134.html

40. Pearson website, http://www.pearsonschool.com/index.cfm?locator=PS1zHe&PMDbSiteId=2781&PMDbSolutionId=6724&PMDbSubSolutionId=&PMDbCategoryId=806&PMDbSubCategoryId=25741&PMDbSubjectAreaId=&PMDbProgramId=76981

41. Pearson Foundation website, http://www.pearsonfoundation.org/pr/20110427-pearson-foundation-partners-with-bill-and-melinda-gates-foundation-to-create-digital-learning-programs.html

42. Smarter Balanced website, http://www.smarterbalanced.org/news/smarter-balanced-and-parcc-to-launch-new-technology-readiness-tool-to-support-transition-to-online-assessments/

43. PARCC website, http://www.parcconline.org/sites/parcc/files/PARCCFAQ_9-18-2013.pdf

44. Singer, A. (2012, September 4). Pearson 'Education'—Who are these people? *Huffington Post*, http://www.huffingtonpost.com/alan-singer/pearson-education-new-york-testing-_b_1850169.html

45. Berliner, D. C., and Glass, G. V. (2014). *50 myths and lies that threaten America's public schools: The real crisis in education.* New York: Teachers College Press.

46. Pegwithpen. Pearson, ALEC, and the brave new (corporate) world; Ravitch. *Reign of error.*

47. Pearson website, http://www.pearsonlearningsolutions.com/school/charters.php

48. Rapoport, A. (2011, September 6). Education Inc. How private companies are profiting from Texas public schools. *The Texas Observer*, http://www.texasobserver.org/the-pearson-graduate/[p. 1].

49. Singer. Pearson 'Education'—Who are these people? [p. 6]

50. Tan, A. (2005). *Saving fish from drowning.* New York: Penguin.

Chapter Twelve

Talking Back to Those Who Want to Destroy Public Education

This chapter offers a set of counternarratives to education reformers' stories of school failure and teacher ineptness. It encourages teachers and other educators to talk back to those who would destroy public education and gives them some words for articulating educational purposes that are forgotten, ignored, or demeaned in the scripted discourse of education reform.

Reform advocates bent on dismantling public education have produced a master narrative based on hyperbole, half-truths, and downright deception. Building on the faulty assumptions laid out in Part I of this book, they have fabricated a story of "crisis and salvation."[1] Schools are in crisis, but reformers are ready with their own special brand of salvation. In collusion with high-profile corporate and political leaders, their well-financed public relations machine has sold America on the discourse of market-based, accountability-driven education reform.

The reformers' story is a melodrama in black and white. The villains are inept teachers who are destroying America's ability to compete in the global marketplace. The heroes are omniscient outsiders who know how to reshape education so that productivity will increase and America will be number one again. The major plot line winds through *A Nation at Risk*, No Child Left Behind, and Race to the Top, building to a crisis point. Then the heroes step in with voucher programs, charter schools, and other private alternatives to the thoroughly discredited public schools. Free-market economic panaceas are ready to save us from a terrible fate.

Teachers and others who want to preserve public schooling in the United States need to challenge the faulty premises on which the reform story is based—that's the point of Part I of this book. But public school proponents also need to shift the ways everyday Americans think and talk about educa-

107

tion. Counternarratives that convey a different story about the vital importance of public education need to be told in ways that capture the attention of ordinary citizens. One way to frame such stories is to highlight purposes of education that go beyond the reformers' obsession with market-based economic explanations for why we need to dismantle public schools.

This chapter describes the elements of four possible counternarratives. Subsections for the chapter are organized around the following purposes for public education: (1) to prepare students for full democratic participation; (2) to maximize every student's human potential; (3) to inspire students to be active learners for life; and (4) to prepare students to improve the world they will inherit.

None of these purposes is presented as supplanting the need for academic knowledge and skills. Indeed, they each rely on rich curriculum, excellent instruction, and informed assessment; but they provide a way for professional educators to "guard the meaning" that is being washed away by the vapid market-based, test-driven agenda of contemporary reform.

COUNTERNARRATIVE 1: PREPARING STUDENTS FOR FULL PARTICIPATION IN OUR DEMOCRACY

When Thomas Jefferson pictured how our new nation would be sustained, he saw the role of an educated populace as vital to the survival of democracy. A government of the people requires an education designed to prepare individuals to participate intelligently in their own governance. Jefferson argued that "the people themselves are [the government's] only safe depositories. And to render even them safe, their minds must be improved."[2] He called for education that would prepare individuals to "perform their duties and protect their rights as citizens."[3]

In Jefferson's day, citizenship was limited to select groups, but the 1800s saw the emergence of "common schools" that had as their expressed purpose the education of a more inclusive democratic citizenry. Horace Mann, father of the common schools movement, built the rationale for providing a publically funded education for everyone on the notion that our republican form of government could not be sustained without an informed citizenry.[4]

During the progressive era of the late nineteenth and early twentieth centuries, John Dewey exemplified the thinking of others of the day who saw inseparable connections between the needs of a democratic society and the purposes of schooling. Dewey believed that a healthy democracy depends on the exercise of intelligence as a way of recognizing and solving problems. He called for schools that fostered the development of intelligent citizens capable of challenging the status quo when it no longer serves a useful purpose and supporting established habits and customs when they prove worthwhile.[5]

In the 1970s, Jacob Bronowski concluded his classic *The Ascent of Man* by warning that if civilization is to survive, a "democracy of the intellect" is essential.[6] He argued that our cultural survival depends on each person's responsible participation in democratic decision making. Bronowski observed what he called a "retreat from knowledge," through which ordinary citizens turn decision making over to specialists. He believed taking knowledge out of the hands of citizens is a recipe for disaster. Bronowski's words are powerful today, and their implications for strong public schools are clear:

> We must not perish by the distance between people and government, between people and power. . . . And that distance can only be conflated, can only be closed, if knowledge sits in the homes and heads of people with no ambition to control others, and not up in the isolated seats of power.[7]

None of these great thinkers was invested in dismantling public schools. They had no interest in reducing the experience of education to prepping for an endless series of tests. Their vision of the teaching-learning process did not include threatening students, teachers, and schools with failure unless they met arbitrary benchmarks based on capricious standards. Their aims for education were not confined to producing efficient workers to power an economic engine that serves the purposes of those who already have the most resources.

Quite the opposite is true. The history of public education in the United States has a consistent theme: schools are in place to prepare all students for full democratic participation. By reasserting the critical importance of this theme, public school advocates can lay claim to a reason for education that makes reformers' narrow perspective on public schools seem myopic and selfish.

Contemporary thinkers who know the deep connections between education and informed democratic participation can help us make our case for the importance of maintaining strong public schools. Jonathan Kozol has warned of the dangerous impact of corporate-driven reform efforts for groups of children who have long been denied equal access to educational opportunity. Kozol has been an articulate spokesperson for the central importance of equitable public education in a democratic society, and he warns of the "niche" effect of charter schools, which "guarantees a swift and vicious deepening of class and racial separation."[8]

Diane Ravitch is an educational historian and outspoken critic of the reform movement. She articulates the importance of public schools in a democratic society as follows:

> Communities and states established public education as a public responsibility in the nineteenth century to educate future citizens and to sustain our democracy. The essential purpose of the public schools, the reason they receive public

funding, is to teach young people the rights and responsibilities of citizens. As citizens, they will be expected to discuss and deliberate issues, to choose our leaders, to take an active role in their communities, and to participate in civic affairs.[9]

Ravitch points out how achieving this purpose is undermined when current reforms reduce the experience of schooling to an obsessive mastery of basic skills in mathematics and reading. She outlines several elements that are critical to informed democratic participation but are ignored or devalued in the reform agenda currently under way, including:

- the ability to read critically, evaluate competing claims, weigh evidence, and come to thoughtful conclusions;
- a solid grounding in history, government, economics, and civics;
- adequate knowledge of science and scientific methods;
- direct exposure to the arts, including great works of fiction; and
- facility with a foreign language.

Ravitch concludes that we cheat children when we focus on routine skills that do not prepare them to participate as full citizens in a democratic society.[10]

It's not just what we teach that prepares students for intelligent participation in our democracy. How we *do* school, what is often called the "hidden curriculum," teaches children at least as much about their place in schools and society as the overt, written-down curriculum.[11] The way school gets done in education settings driven by the reform agenda teaches students that their purpose for being in school is to produce certain outcomes that will allow them to progress to the next station on the education assembly line.

Charter schools such as KIPP that have been held up as exemplars of what's possible when charters replace public schools hardly prepare young people for participation as full citizens in a democracy. In fact, parents and students have to sign contracts agreeing to comply with the program's rigid expectations or be removed.[12] The lesson is that success is tied to figuring out how to satisfy those who have power over your future—a mind-set that's perfect for many forms of government, but not for democracy as Jefferson saw it.

Blind compliance and meeting the expectations of more powerful others are not the stuff of informed democratic participation, but these are defining characteristics of the kind of schooling sold by reform hucksters. The links between public schools and preparation for full citizenship in a democracy are built into the fabric of our society. We need to remind the public, the media, and those responsible for making policy that a piece of our democratic way of life is threatened when public education is sacrificed on the altar of private interests.

Our story of the purpose of education should highlight the historical place of schooling as a public good. Schools are central to community identity and social cohesion. In Ravitch's words, as a citizen, "You recognize that the school is educating the children of the community and that this is good for everyone. . . . You think of public education as an institution that educates citizens, future voters, members of your community."[13]

Education is not a commodity to be bought and sold. Every American has the right to a free public education. That education should include experiences that allow students to practice the tenets of democracy and apply the principles of informed decision making. When schooling is packaged for profit, efficiency in mastering skills takes the place of the deep involvement required to produce thoughtful decision makers.

The purpose of education has to be larger than producing workers and consumers to fuel a competitive economy. These economic aims are meaningless unless future generations are also prepared to enact their responsibilities as citizens. Thoughtful, engaged future citizens need a rich, broad curriculum that includes much more than facility with selected reading and math skills.

Citizens of the future need to see education as a meaningful experience that has value because they are being prepared to exercise the rights and responsibilities of democratic decision makers. Citizens of today need to be reminded that public schools are a historical expression of the public will to prepare children for full democratic participation.

Instead of being the liability they are portrayed to be by those who want to do away with them, public schools should be seen as one of America's greatest assets. The historical success of our democratic way of life is intimately tied to public schooling in the United States. Indeed, if those who are orchestrating the attack on public education win the day, one of the long-term casualties may turn out to be democracy itself.

COUNTERNARRATIVE 2: MAXIMIZING EVERY STUDENT'S HUMAN POTENTIAL

Virtually all public schools have a mission statement that is meant to guide everything that happens in and around the school. Most of these statements of purpose include sentences like the following:

- We are committed to providing all children with optimal educational opportunities so that they can reach their full potential.
- We strive to educate the whole child.

- We provide programs that enable students to develop physically, emotionally, socially, and academically.

The individuals who put together mission statements like these believe that the purpose of public schooling goes well beyond preparing the next-generation labor force. In their hearts, most teachers are committed to tenets like those listed, but what they are being forced to do to meet the demands being foisted on them by outside forces makes it appear that aims like maximizing human potential in every child have gone by the wayside.

An obsession with test scores and accountability leaves out way more of what it means to be human than it includes. Each of the statements of educational mission above is expanded below to sketch an alternative picture of the purpose of education, one based on public education's potential to support all of America's children in their quest to become fully functioning human beings.

We are committed to providing all children with optimal educational opportunities so that they can reach their full potential. Notice that the phrasing stipulates "all children." Unlike most private and charter schools, public schools take in every child who shows up at the door. No matter their background, language, experience, or disability status, no students are turned away. Public schools don't just admit those who will raise their profiles, profits, and portfolios; public education is in place to enhance the life chances of *all children.*

Helping all children reach their "full potential" first of all means giving them opportunities to explore possibilities and discover their own potential. The way that reformers are shaping schools means that human potential is being essentialized in the form of test scores. Students (and teachers and schools) are being sorted into categories that circumscribe what's possible based on mere numbers.

Students are not numbers. They are complex human beings, each with a unique array of capacities, experiences, and dreams. One of the outcomes of releasing public education from the shackles of the reform agenda would be the opportunity to focus on the development of those capacities, build on those experiences, and nurture those dreams.

The purpose of schooling ought not to be to sort children into categories to make the system appear to be efficient (and, many would say, to reproduce the socially stratified status quo).[14] Schools ought to be places that challenge children to explore what it means to be a fully realized human being, to have a hand in determining what it would take to reach their full potential, and to be given opportunities to work in every way possible to realize that potential.

We strive to educate the whole child. The factory model that reformers use to characterize schooling collapses when we stop thinking of children as products to be mass-produced on an assembly line. Business concepts like net operating margin, economy of scale, and return on investment are absurd when applied to the lives of young human beings. Children are not a set of components to be assembled as efficiently and cheaply as possible. Education that ignores the wholeness of human experience distorts reality and devalues children.

When statements of school philosophy proclaim the goal of educating the "whole child," they signal a commitment to providing a broad set of experiences that address more than just the academic progress of each child. As was established in Part I of this book, the reform agenda's emphasis on testing reading and mathematics has narrowed the curriculum in significant ways;[15] and first to be pushed out are music, art, physical education, and other areas of the curriculum from which students derive a sense of balance, perspective, and satisfaction.

It's not just the written-down curriculum that gets narrowed with the business-driven model reformers want to force on schools. The joy of experiencing life as a child is also threatened. As Ravitch points out, "Devotees of the business approach like to say, 'You measure what you treasure.' Believing this, they have fastened a pitiless regime of testing on the nation's schools that now reaches down as low as kindergarten." Ravitch laments this appropriation of childhood experience, noting that children need nurturing and opportunities to play, not more testing.[16]

As we resist the takeover of public education, we need to remind everyone of what we treasure. We treasure the whole child. Yes, we accept responsibility for the cognitive development of all our children, but we want that dimension of development to include more than what's measured on selected items on certain tests. Yes, we accept responsibility for preparing students for productive futures, but we want them also to learn about the elements of experience that make life worth living.

We provide programs that enable students to develop physically, emotionally, socially, and academically. Teachers who are carefully prepared in well-established teacher education programs learn that the complexity of children's development involves interrelationships among different domains. Children have a difficult time learning when their physical, emotional, and social needs are not being met.[17] To pretend that children's academic development is not impacted by other developmental domains is pure folly; yet, emotional, social, and physical development are virtually ignored in contemporary reform.

In fact, when issues with children's health, emotional security, and social well-being are identified as factors contributing to children's low performance on tests and other measures of school progress, reformers claim that educators are making excuses and not expecting enough of their students.[18] Ignoring the impact of children's physical, emotional, and social development on their learning potential is like factory managers assuming that it does not matter what raw materials are used in the production of their product.

Dedicated teachers know the power of high expectations, but they also recognize the responsibility they have to address children's needs across developmental domains. Providing programs that enable students to develop more than just academically is a way not just to improve academic outcomes, it is another way to improve children's chances of maximizing their human potential.

When individuals describe their reasons for selecting teaching as a career, they do not proclaim their commitment to the economy; they talk about touching human lives and making a difference in society. [19] When successful teachers say why they stay in education, they don't describe their successes in terms of producing workers; they talk about the satisfaction of helping young people discover their potential and fulfill their dreams. [20]

Contrast these dispositions for making life better for children and society with the goals of market-based reform advocates. A powerful example of the ways that corporate types think about children is captured in this quote (complete with capital letters) from a presentation used to attract investment in educational reform enterprises: "All students are not equal; SOME ARE MORE PROFITABLE THAN OTHERS." [21] Arguing that we are committed to maximizing every student's human potential has to be seen as the high ground when our enemies think of children as profitable (or not) commodities.

COUNTERNARRATIVE 3: INSPIRING STUDENTS TO BE ACTIVE LEARNERS FOR LIFE

"Preparing lifelong learners" is a hackneyed phrase. It is overused to the point that its meaning has been all but forgotten. But that meaning is vital to understanding the value of public education for every child. Our capacity to learn is a quality that makes humans unique in the animal kingdom. When our enormous potential as learners is reduced to an obsessive focus on preparing for the next standards-based assessment, we are blurring connections to our own humanness.

It is possible to think of learning as the central purpose of school. [22] Learning can be conceived of as an inherently valuable human activity. Schools can be organized and run based on the notion that learning is students' and teachers' reason for being there. Curriculum can be developed that gives students opportunities to experience the pure joy of learning for its own sake. Instruction can be facilitated that helps students discover the inherent value of learning and the satisfaction of seeing themselves as able learners.

Assessments can be devised that measure how well students are developing as active learners.

The learning described here is not part of the reform agenda. In fact, when the reason for being in school is reduced to meeting the accountability expectations of reform advocates, learning becomes nothing more than a means to an end. It takes on only secondary, instrumental value, and learning's inherent value is lost. Worse, what is to be learned in accountability-driven schools is so circumscribed and so isolated from meaningful experience that students just go through the motions, never getting the chance to experience the exhilaration of learning as an inherently valuable human activity.

Researchers make a useful distinction between performance goals and learning goals.[23] When students operate within systems based on performance goals, they focus on doing whatever is necessary to avoid failure at the next task put before them. In contrast, those who have internalized an ethos based on learning goals are interested in improving their own capacities as learners. The former group avoids risks that may expose their incompetence, which sometimes means giving up entirely. The latter group thrives on challenging situations that provide opportunities for growth.

Carol Dweck, a pioneer in describing the processes of learning motivation, notes that all children are born with an intense desire to learn. Young children are not afraid to make mistakes. They learn complex skills like walking and talking by barging ahead, learning from their errant tries and exalting in their small victories.[24] But when virtually everything in schools is based on improving performance, children's natural inclinations to learn and love learning are quickly socialized away.

Dweck cites sociologist and political theorist Benjamin Barber, who avers: "I don't divide the world into the weak and the strong, or the successes and the failures, those who make it or those who don't. I divide the world into learners and non-learners."[25] Like others, Barber believes that the stability of our increasingly complex world depends on people's capacity to learn. Schools that emphasize performance on arbitrary assessments at the expense of meaningful experiences are creating a generation of nonlearners.

Nonlearners may be just what the reform advocates have in mind. If their goal is to maintain the vastly inequitable economic status quo we are experiencing today, then producing compliant workers with low-level basic skills may be just the ticket. But, if schooling is about more than engineering a passive labor pool, then a generation of learners is what's needed. Strong, well-supported public schools with strong, well-prepared teachers are critical to reawakening a generation of learners.

Those of us who want to push back against the manic drive to institute school reform based on performance-based outcome measures need to remind our potential supporters of the importance of learning processes in a genuine education. Their experience in school teaches students what's valued there and socializes them to internalize those values. When outcomes in the form of test scores are what really count, then how you learn and how you think of yourself as a learner don't matter.

Reformers like to claim that they are advocates of evidence-based practices, while they berate those who oppose them as relying on approaches that are not based on solid research. But overwhelming evidence from brain researchers, cognitive scientists, education researchers, and other social scientists shows that focusing on the processes of learning is vital to helping children learn how to learn and how to think of themselves as able learners.[26]

Learners, as opposed to nonlearners, see learning as a challenging set of cognitive and metacognitive activities that are within their reach. They are capable of being intentional about their own learning; that is, they can monitor their thinking and learn to apply strategies to improve the quality of that thinking.[27] An education that fosters intentional learning sends the message to children that the processes of learning are what count.

Children's perceptions of themselves as active learners have to be nurtured, and their attempts to learn how to learn have to be scaffolded by smart, dedicated teachers.[28] When teachers' careers depend on the efficient generation of products in the form of test scores, a focus on the processes that make learning a meaningful human activity that has inherent value is close to impossible. When children are socialized into a world that values performance goals over learning goals, their opportunities to become lifetime learners are all but lost.

Four teachers were invited to lunch by President Obama in the summer of 2014. One of those teachers, Justin Minkel, posted his reaction to the meeting, in which he reported telling the president that "the creativity, curiosity, and sense of wonder that make students such a joy to teach has been stripped from students' experience [in schools] desperate to raise test scores." Minkel concluded that we need to give teachers the autonomy to restore the "delight" in teaching and learning.[29] Without joy and delight in the classroom, lifelong learning is an empty phrase.

It bears repeating that none of the politicians, business moguls, entrepreneurs, or philanthropists behind the education reform movement would send their own children to the kinds of institutions they advocate for other people's children. You can be sure that the children of these movers and shakers are being taught to think and learn and to value themselves as thinkers and learners. It's certain that the processes of becoming a thinker and learner drive the curriculum, teaching, and assessment practices of the elite private schools they attend.

Reform advocates should know what it means to be an active learner for life. They should know that a rich, full education experience is much more than mastering a set of arbitrary performance standards. They should know that being a nonlearner puts individuals at a sustained disadvantage from early childhood through adulthood. They should know that learning has its own inherent worth. They should know that learning how to learn is critical to individual development and social stability.

It is our job as teachers, educators, and public school supporters to send the message that inspiring students to become active learners for life is a much more important goal than engineering students to become compliant workers. If an ethos that values a rich and deep conceptualization of learning is what's expected for the schooling of reform advocates' children, we need to ask why we would expect anything less for all our children.

COUNTERNARRATIVE 4: PREPARING STUDENTS TO IMPROVE THE WORLD THEY WILL INHERIT

In 1932, George S. Counts boldly asked, *Dare the school build a new social order?*[30] Counts was one of the first to make visible the social, cultural, and political purposes of schooling. He challenged educators to acknowledge the inescapably political nature of their work, and he described approaches to education designed to prepare students to work positively to reconstruct society.

The social reconstruction movement that Counts help found never gained traction in the political climate of the day, but his basic premise that schools have an obligation to prepare students to improve the world in which they will live still rings true. While contemporary proponents of what is often called a critical perspective on the purposes of schooling are often painted as radicals (as was Counts in his day), the reconstructionist dictum that teachers "cannot evade the responsibility of participating actively in the task of reconstituting the democratic tradition and of thus working positively toward a new society"[31] remains salient.

Many elements of the social order that needed reconstitution in the 1930s are echoed in the social, economic, and political circumstances of the 2010s. Individuals with wealth and power are becoming wealthier and more powerful, while those with the fewest resources and least political capital are steadily losing ground.[32] Dare contemporary educators make the claim that a legitimate purpose of schooling is to prepare students to help shape a new, more equitable social order?

It's certain that the rich and powerful individuals at the helm of the reform movement will not see helping students see the structural inequalities built into a system that advantages the rich and powerful as a reasonable purpose of education. In fact, the fabric of the reform initiatives this book seeks to debunk depends on an uncritical acceptance of the social and economic status quo. Privatization and other market-based approaches represent the essence of what keeps rich people rich, so giving students tools for challenging those approaches would be unthinkable to education reformers.

School experiences designed to prepare students to improve the world have their contemporary roots in the transformative pedagogical approaches of Paolo Freire. Bringing literacy to Brazilian peasants, Freire argued against what he called a banking concept of education, wherein teachers make deposits into the passive minds of students. He demonstrated that lives and societies can be improved through the processes of consciousness raising, critical reading of the world, and taking action. [33]

Building on Freire's foundational ideas, teachers who take a critical perspective see knowledge as historically and politically situated and teach in ways that challenge traditional approaches to passing along cultural knowledge as if it were absolute truth. Their approaches focus on raising learners' consciousness, providing tools for critically analyzing texts and social conditions, and working together to challenge power structures that are unfair to many individuals and groups. [34]

Schools that see preparing students to create a better world as an important purpose for education have rigorous content coverage and high expectations. They value high-quality curriculum and excellent teaching. They expect their students to know as much or more than "banking model" schools; but they want students' knowledge to be acquired within a context that teaches them how to think critically about what they are learning and how it impacts themselves and others in the world.

This kind of educational purpose acknowledges that the world children will inherit will look different from the past in more ways than we can imagine. Transformative pedagogical approaches prepare students to assess and protect what's valuable at the same time they critique and resist what's harmful. Their studies have meaning beyond preparing for the next standardized test. Their reason for being in school is to give them tools for shaping the destiny of the planet.

When education reform advocates fabricate the rationale for why we need to drastically alter public schooling, they always cite US students' performance on international tests as evidence that we are losing ground. It does not matter that their assertions are suspect (see Part I), the message is always that we need to fix our broken schools to compete in the global economy. The trouble is their fixes narrow the experiences of students and poorly prepare future citizens for intelligent participation in shaping a rapidly shrinking world.

Education that develops individuals who have the capacity to actively shape the future is the antithesis of what reformers want for public schools. Indeed, a truly transformative curriculum would include a careful examination of what public schools are for, what is taught there and why, who benefits and does not from the ways things are done, and what other possibilities exist. Students would be challenged to step back from the experience of being a student to understand the purposes behind what they are asked to do in school.

Schools whose purpose is defined by the obsession to raise test scores would not fare well when questions about what schools are for are asked. Reformers would have a hard time justifying their market-driven approaches when responding to questions about who benefits and who does not. Just doing what has been done unsuccessfully in the past, only doing it harder and longer, would not be satisfactory responses to questions about what possibilities exist for getting better.

Patrick Finn points out that children of the rich have always received what he calls an *empowering* education, while the children of those without wealth and power get a *domesticating* education. The goals of domesticating education are to make a person "productive and dependable, but not troublesome."[35] Reformers want nothing less than empowering education for their own children, but their formulas for public school change look like the master plan for domesticating the rest of us.

Is it the schools' place to encourage students to critique their worlds and the worlds around them? Do careful analyses of the social, political, and economic realities that shape the world have a place in schooling? Dare the schools participate in preparing students to build a new social order? Remembering Counts's axiom that teaching is an inescapably political act, many would argue that when we don't provide the kind of transformative, empowering education outlined here, we are playing into the hands of the reform agenda and tacitly teaching future citizens that doing what more powerful others tell us, no matter its impact, is what counts in school and beyond.

All children deserve an educational experience that empowers them to act intelligently in the world. All children deserve a public school education that enables them to critically examine their place in society. All children deserve the tools needed to make judgments about what is working and what is not, who is thriving and who is not, and what is possible and what is not. Schools whose purpose is to empower and enable students in these ways have a legitimate place in considerations about what kinds of schools we want in the future.

The four counternarratives outlined here are not the only possibilities. These are examples of stories educators and public school advocates need to be telling to interrupt the reform tale that is incessantly told and retold to political decision makers and the general public. Joe Kincheloe described how contemporary reformers have created a new "commonsense" in American discourse. He called on educators to expose this commonsense as "oppressive, bellicose, and exclusive."[36] We can interrupt what is taken for granted by offering alternative purposes for public schooling that are liberating, reasoned, and inclusive.

The narratives we use to counter the melodramas of reform advocates need to emphasize the contributions that pubic schools make to the general good. Our stories need to highlight the importance of public education to the millions of individuals whose life chances are directly related to what happens in school. Our reasons for being need to signal our commitment to improving all the communities we serve and the overall society we share. Our narratives need to establish our resolve to guard the meaning that reform initiatives systematically strip away.

Teachers have to be guardians of meaning; otherwise, future generations will be socialized to think of education as little more than perpetually spitting back inert ideas on tests imposed by powerful unseen others. Public school advocates have to work hard to bring meaning to the reform debate; otherwise, the business model promoted by their opponents will win the day.

The alternative narratives proposed here are not perfect, but they don't pretend to be. What educational purposes like these add to the education discourse is a thoughtful consideration of what is meaningful—for children, for schools, for society. Preparing students for full democratic participation, maximizing their human potential, inspiring them to be active learners for life, and preparing them to improve the world they will inherit have to carry more meaning than reformers' aims to make a profit at the same time they produce efficient, compliant workers.

NOTES

1. Zeichner, K., and Pena-Sandoval, C. (2015). Venture philanthropy and teacher education policy in the U.S.: The role of the New Schools Venture Fund. *Teachers College Record*, *117*(6), http://www.tcrecord.org/Content.asp?ContentId=17539 [p. 3]

2. From Thomas Jefferson's "Notes on the state of Virginia," quoted in Butts, R. F. (1980). *The revival of civic learning*. Bloomington, IN: Phi Delta Kappa Educational Foundation. [p. 55]

3. Wagoner, L. J. (1976). Thomas Jefferson and the education of a new nation. Bloomington, IN: Phi Delta Kappa Fastback # 73. [p. 25]

4. Mann, H. (1872). *Annual reports on education*. Boston: Lee and Shepard.

5. Dewey, J. (1966). *Democracy and education*. New York: The Free Press.

6. Bronowski, J. (1973). *The ascent of man*. New York: Little, Brown and Company. See also, Hatch, J. A., and Conrath, J. M. (1988). Refocusing the identity of schooling: Education for a democracy of the intellect. *Kappa Delta Pi Record*, *24*(1), 41–45.

7. Bronowski. *The ascent of man*. [p. 434]

8. Cody, A. (2011, July 18). Confronting the inequality juggernaut: A q and a with Jonathan Kozol. *Education Week*, http://blogs.edweek.org/teachers/living-in-dialogue/2011/07/time_to_get_off_our_knees_why.html

9. Ravitch, D. (2013). *Reign of error: The hoax of the privatization movement and the danger to America's public schools*. New York: Alfred A. Knopf. [p. 237]

10. Ravitch. *Reign of error*.

11. Jackson, P. W. (1990). *Life in classrooms*. New York: Teachers College Press.

12. Goodman, J. F. (2013). Charter management organizations and the regulated environment: Is it worth the price? *Educational Researcher, 42*(2), 89–96.

13. Ravitch. *Reign of error.* [p. 311]

14. Anyon, J. (2005). *Radical possibilities: Public policy, urban education, and a new social movement.* New York: Teachers College Press.

15. Hatch, J. A. (2002). Accountability shovedown: Resisting the standards movement in early childhood education. *Phi Delta Kappan, 83*(6), 457–462.

16. Ravitch. *Reign of error.* [p. 303]

17. Maslow, A. H. (1954). *Motivation and personality.* New York: Harper.

18. Kumashiro, K. K. (2012). *Bad teacher: How blaming teachers distorts the bigger picture.* New York: Teachers College Press.

19. Hatch, J. A. (2006). Pre-service teachers' reasons for selecting urban teaching. *2006 Yearbook of Urban Learning, Teaching, and Research,* 4–10.

20. Nieto, S. (2003). *What keeps teachers going?* New York: Teachers College Press.

21. Parthenon Group. (2009). Investing in education: Where are the opportunities and how can you capture them? http://www.parthenon.com/GetFile.aspx?u=%2fLists%2fThoughtLeadership%2fAttachments%2f4%2fParthenon%2520Perspectives_Investing%2520in%2520Education.pdf [p. 13]

22. Hatch, J. A. (2005). *Teaching in the new kindergarten.* Clifton Park, NY: Delmar.

23. Dweck, C. S. (1999). *Self-theories: Their role in motivation, personality and development.* Philadelphia: Psychology Press.

24. Dweck, C. S. (2006). *Mindset: The new psychology of success.* New York: Random House.

25. Dweck. *Mindset.* [p. 16]

26. Bransford, J. D., Brown, A. L., and Cocking, R. R. (Eds.). (2000). *How people learn: Brain, mind, experience, and school.* Washington, DC: National Academy Press.

27. Bransford, Brown and Cocking. *How people learn.*

28. Hatch, J. A. (2010). Rethinking the relationship between learning and development: Teaching for learning in early childhood classrooms. *The Educational Forum, 74,* 258–268.

29. Strauss, V. (2014, July 10). What 4 teachers told Obama over lunch. *Washington Post,* http://www.washingtonpost.com/blogs/answer-sheet/wp/2014/07/10/what-4-teachers-told-obama-over-lunch/ [p. 1]

30. Counts, G.S. (1932) *Dare the school build a new social order?* New York: John Day Company.

31. Progressive Education Association Committee on Social and Economic Problems. (1933). *A call to the teachers of the nation.* New York: John Day Company. [p. 31]

32. Lowrey, A. (2013, September 10). The rich get richer through the recovery. *New York Times,* http://economix.blogs.nytimes.com/2013/09/10/the-rich-get-richer-through-the-recovery/?_php=true percent _type=blogs percent _r=0

33. Freire, P. (1970). *Pedagogy of the oppressed.* New York: Continuum.

34. Souto-Manning, M. (2010). *Freire, teaching and learning: Culture circles across contexts.* New York: Peter Lang.

35. Finn, P. J. (1999). *Literacy with an attitude: Educating working-class children in their own self-interest.* Albany, NY: State University of New York Press. [pp. ix–x]

36. Kincheloe, J. L. (2009). Contextualizing the madness: A critical analysis of the assault on teacher education and schools. In S. L. Groenke and J. A. Hatch (Eds.), *Critical pedagogy and teacher education in the neoliberal era: Small openings.* New York: Springer. [p. 34]

Chapter Thirteen

Strategies for Reclaiming Our Profession

This concluding chapter is framed by Winston Churchill's World War II dictum: "If you are going through hell, keep going." Teachers are surely going through hell because of the radical reforms that are being forced on public education in the United States. Teachers and public school advocates can give up and let those with the most power and least insight reform schooling so it works like a giant business enterprise, or we can keep going—finding ways to reclaim our profession and save public education.

This chapter builds on the purpose stories in chapter 12 and offers educators ways to fight through the hell they are going through. Headings for chapter subsections include the following: (1) Talk Back to the Forces Out to Destroy the Teaching Profession; (2) Speak Up About What's Best for Children; (3) Speak Up About What's Best for Our Society; (4) Don't Participate in Your Own Degradation; (5) Engage in Union Activities That Protect the Profession; (6) Join with Others to Influence Public Opinion and Education Policy Making; and (7) Take the High Ground, Guard the Meaning, Redefine High-Quality Education.

The chapter includes examples of how the suggestions presented have been enacted by individuals and groups who are fighting for our profession. Also included are references to specific resources (e.g., websites, organizations, blogs, books, articles) that support teachers' efforts to protect public schooling and reclaim our professional status.

TALK BACK TO THE FORCES OUT TO DESTROY THE TEACHING PROFESSION

Those who are working to radically change the face of public education in America understand very well that the more negative images of teachers and schools they can put before the pubic the better their chances of succeeding. It does not matter how far-fetched or one-sided their stories of school failure are, their sound bites and press releases stay on message. And the media pass the propaganda along as if it were legitimate news.

This book is about talking back—speaking truth to power. As teachers, we are in a vulnerable spot when we defend ourselves and our profession. Because we are public employees with very little power, we risk being labeled as "troublemakers," punished in subtle and not-so-subtle ways, or even faced with dismissal for insubordination if we speak too loudly.[1] As support from our unions has been stripped away by the same forces we are trying to resist, talking about the negative consequences of unjust reform efforts has become even more risky.

But teachers all over the country are speaking out. They are making their voices heard in neighborhoods and communities, in the news media, the professional literature, cyberspace, and the halls of government. More and more educators are telling our side of the story in ways that challenge the master narrative of those who are out to destroy public education. All of us who care about preserving and improving an education system that reflects the democratic values on which the United States was founded need to find our own voice and join the chorus of dissent.

We need to rediscover our capacity to "be outraged by outrageous things" and speak out against the "top-down, corporate-style mandates that are squeezing the life out of classrooms."[2] Yes, it takes courage. But, it can be done, and it can make a difference. What follows are several examples of educators from all across the nation taking a stand and speaking truth to power. Each provides a sample of what is possible and a model for enacting resistance that exposes the outrageous propositions at the core of contemporary education reform efforts.

In Knoxville, Tennessee, Lauren Hopson, a veteran third-grade teacher, made a powerful speech to the Knox County Board of Education.[3] She articulated the frustration of her fellow teachers with endless top-down mandates from state and local leaders for expanded testing and more rigorous teacher evaluation. The video of her speech was uploaded to YouTube,[4] where it had over 100,000 views in a matter of weeks. Other Knox County teachers have been inspired by Hopson's bravery and several have taken the microphone at board meetings, while others have worn red to the meetings to show their solidarity.[5]

High school teachers at Garfield High School in Seattle, Washington, received national attention when they unanimously voted to refuse to give the Measures of Academic Achievement test in 2013. Administrators at first threatened to fire teachers for insubordination if they refused to give the tests, but later backed down as boycotting teachers made their case to parents, the community, and those watching from around the country. Teachers led this grassroots resistance, they formed close collaborative relationships with parents and students, and they offered alternative solutions to the testing policies they were opposing.[6]

Other school-wide acts of resistance in response to the implementation of oppressive reform policies have received less national attention but offer more evidence of what's possible when educators band together. For example, the faculties of two schools in New York City took a stand on separate issues. When PS 24 was told that NYC schools would be adding "periodic assessment tests" to their already packed testing regime, the principal and teachers refused to administer the new tests, arguing for alternative assessments that made sense for their students.[7] When a merit pay scheme based on student test scores was proposed, a Brooklyn elementary school staff stood together and voted not to participate in a program they saw as unproven, unfair, and divisive.[8]

Small groups of dedicated teachers have found ways to successfully resist arbitrary reform measures in their schools. In Chicago, for example, twelve high school teachers wrote a letter refusing to administer a counterproductive test. The letter led to meetings with school and local government officials, which attracted the attention of the press. These brave teachers provided evidence for the inability of the test to improve student performance and refused to back down when threatened with termination. When the system made the decision to discontinue using the test system-wide, one of the leaders of the protest reflected, "We never expected to win; we only expected to fight. Isn't that what we should teach our students every day?"[9]

New York City teachers who were disgusted with the ways teachers and schools were portrayed in the popular film *Waiting for Superman* produced their own film about the realities of the current reform movement. Entitled *The Inconvenient Truth Behind Waiting for Superman*, the film highlights the real-life experiences of public school teachers, students, and parents to show how the reforms valorized in the original film actually harm public education. So far, over 100,000 people have viewed the teachers' film, and thousands of copies have been mailed to supporters around the globe.[10]

Teachers from across the United States are writing editorials through which they can express their unhappiness with current educational reform and attract support from colleagues, the general public, and policy makers. Sadly, many powerful editorials are being penned by teachers who are resigning from the profession because they were being forced to implement policies that are not "good for kids,"[11] one saying she could no longer justify being "part of a broken system that was causing damage to those very children I was there to serve."[12]

Other educators have produced articles for professional publications and written blogs as ways to make evident the negative consequences of radical reform for students, teachers, and society. For example, Texas teacher Vivian Maguire published a piece in *Education Week* that asked, "Is anybody listening to teachers?"[13] and Vermont principal Keri Gelenian posted a comment that was picked up by education bloggers entitled "The wrong choices on standards."[14] (Appendix B of this book includes an annotated list of organizations, websites, and blogs that support and give voice to educator resistance.)

John Kuhn, former teacher and current school administer from Texas, has published a book based on his experiences resisting "the attack on public education."[15] Kuhn has also produced editorials that have received widespread distribution on the Internet[16] and made speeches that have gone viral on YouTube.[17] His work lays bare the scare tactics behind the reform movement and offers fellow educators a brave example of standing up for what's right for children.

These examples demonstrate that resisting those out to destroy public education is possible on many fronts. Educators can utilize traditional and social media to make their perspectives known, they can act individually and in concert with others, and they can put the spotlight on a variety of local and global issues impacting the future of public education.

It is telling and important that all of the cited publications for the exemplary acts of resistance outlined above were authored by current or former educators. Talking back to the forces out to destroy public education is not the job of a small group of select spokespersons; it is the work of us all.

John Kuhn highlights ways each of us can get involved in the struggle to save public education:

> Learn about the issues and use your teacher voice, parent voice, or student voice. Write letters to the editor of your local paper if you are so inclined. Post commentaries and links to relevant journalism on Twitter or Facebook. Tell your friends. Fight the reform wars in the comments sections of reform-friendly blogs. Challenge misconceptions and deliberate mendacity when you have the chance. Spread the news each time public schools do something well, and spread the news each time yet another reform initiative is proven fraudulent.[18]

SPEAK UP ABOUT WHAT'S BEST FOR CHILDREN

When we talk back to the powerful forces that are demeaning our profession and destroying our schools, we need to emphasize the direct negative impact reformers' free-market solutions have on children and society. As has been made clear throughout this book, teachers have been singled out as the primary target in the war on public education. That we need to defend ourselves is evident; but we can do that most effectively by helping others see that the policies and practices of educational reform are harmful to children and a threat to society.

Albert Einstein is given credit for the maxim "Not everything that can be counted counts, and not everything that counts can be counted." Reforms driven by the logic of standards-based accountability assume that what can be easily counted is all that counts, and they ignore the fact that what counts most cannot be counted at all. Scores on standardized tests are the bread and butter of education reform. They provide a proxy for achievement, but for all the reasons laid out in Part I, they don't even give us a good estimate of what was really learned. More problematic, they cannot assess what counts most in a child's development in school.

Children are not reducible to numbers. Children are multifaceted, complex individuals with strengths and weaknesses, hopes and fears, capacities for greatness and anxieties about failure. Classrooms are not assembly lines. Classrooms are multilayered, complex social settings in which young people explore their roles as learners, discover their capacities as human beings, and locate their places in society and the world. Making test scores for accountability what counts in school sends the clear signal that students are reducible to numbers and the complexity of their humanity is not what counts.

As educators responsible for making school happen within the complexities of classrooms, we need to speak out against the endless cycle of testing and more testing to prepare for testing. We need to resist accountability regimes that erase the humanity of our students. We need to let others know that reform efforts based on improving test scores harm children's chances of developing into fully functioning individuals because they keep us from seeing children as humans "reaching for empathy, for uncertainty, for knowing that this lived experience cannot be measured."[19]

The real consequences of the accountability-based reform agenda for children have been clearly identified by teachers. Chris Whitney describes how the pressure of testing literally makes children sick in his classroom. He offers his alternative to mindlessly getting kids ready for tests:

> I want kids to feel the joy of being alive, I want kids to sing out in the middle of class "just because," I want kids to laugh, cry, and hold each other when things get hard, I want kids to know they are not alone, and I want kids to feel love. Most of all, I just want to teach the joy of living. . . . [A]nd state testing does not have any place in that vision.[20]

Peter Greene rejects the emphasis on competition that drives policies like Race to the Top. He points out the irony of business moguls like Bill Gates championing competition as a way to reach excellence when they have historically done all they can to limit other businesses' ability to compete. Greene says,

> Racing is a terrible awful no good very bad metaphor for what should be happening in schools. [Teachers] are not racers. We are builders. And building takes time and care and attention. And every beam, every bolt, every square inch of surface matters. Every aspect of the building rests on and supports other aspects. And if you build a great building next to mine, it does not diminish me, but adds to my work. [21]

Pauline Hawkins notes the decline in student morale over her eleven years of teaching, with direct reference to the implementation of NCLB mandates. She tells how her students have lost their "sense of pride in who they were and self-confidence in who they would become someday." She describes her efforts to help children see that education is not meant to be punitive, but the only way they can improve their lives. She laments:

> The truth is the current educational system is punishing them for their inadequacies, rather than helping them discover their unique talents; our educational system is failing our children because it is not meeting their needs. [22]

Even students who do well on standardized tests are being limited by the reform agenda's obsession with this narrow view of accountability. When what can be counted becomes what counts, children are not taught to think for themselves but are programmed to generate right answers to standard prompts. Learning for its own sake is devalued when what is rewarded is convergence on the single correct response. And the goal of becoming a lifelong learner is ignored when even the most capable students are focused on mastering the prescribed content on the next standardized assessment. [23]

Further, when systems are pressured to meet arbitrary goals on annual assessments of student progress, they are forced to practice a kind of educational *triage*, putting time and resources into improving the test performance of "bubble kids" who are just below proficiency levels. Thus, children who are already proficient are assumed to be fine without special attention, and those so far behind they are not likely to measure at proficient are written off as not worthy of the effort. [24]

Schools are not field hospitals where who gets treated and who does not depends on who is most likely to survive. Providing an education for all of America's children is the core mission of public schools. That mission is threatened by accountability policies that systematically label children, schools, and teachers as failures not worthy of saving. Educators need to speak up about the implications of these and other reform policies that threaten the life chances of our children and ultimately undermine the foundations of our democratic society.

SPEAK UP ABOUT WHAT'S BEST FOR OUR SOCIETY

Education reformers who want to turn public schools over to private interests operate within the mindset of neoliberalism. Building on the economic theories of Friedrich von Hayek and his student Milton Friedman and popularized in the novels of Ayn Rand, neoliberals (who prefer to call themselves libertarians) believe in unfettered capitalism, unregulated competition, and unlimited privatization.

Neoliberals work from the assumption that government regulation is inherently bad whenever it limits the free flow of competitive forces. They see survival of the fittest as an appropriate outcome for the application of their policies.[25] Free-market approaches to educational reform evolved within the larger context of neoliberal economic applications in the United States and around the world. Deregulation, union busting, and trickle-down economics represent neoliberal victories from the last century; and collapsing markets, high unemployment rates, and ever-increasing inequality between the rich and poor are the twenty-first-century legacy of those victories.

Notions like Rand's proposition that selfishness is the highest of moral virtues and that the masses are parasites living off the hard work of capitalists[26] have become part of the normative thinking of conservative elements in the US political system, witness Paul Ryan's budget proposals and Mitt Romney's statements about the 47 percent. Still, neoliberal principles are almost never challenged by mainstream politicians on either side of the aisle.

Critics point out that neoliberals and the wealthy individuals who benefit from their policies have spent hundreds of millions of dollars to make "neoliberalism seem as if it were the natural and normal condition of mankind." Neoliberals have created a "huge network of foundations, institutes, research centers, publications, scholars, writers and public relations hacks to develop, package and push their ideas and doctrine relentlessly."[27] Anyone who challenges the ethos of letting the competitive marketplace determine the fate of human beings and not the other way around is labeled as socialist, unAmerican, or worse.

Within the ascension of the neoliberal worldview, it makes perfect sense that schooling, one of the largest sources of public spending, would be a logical target for privatization. If supporters of public schooling are going to be able to make the case for why we need to maintain public schools in the United States, we must be able to counter the neoliberal arguments for applying market-based approaches to education. We need to point out how these *and who goes to private schools ch.12*

approaches hurt children at the same time they offer a real threat to our democratic society.

As was detailed in Part I, school privatization efforts have unfolded on many fronts, from vouchers and charter schools to alternative teacher licensure schemes. If the goal is to take all the money spent on public education and turn it over to private enterprise, then the profit incentives for private enterprise are enormous; but what are the consequences for the rest of us of allowing market forces to determine what the educational experiences of all Americans will look like?

We already have a good idea. We will see more closures of public schools that will leave those communities with the least political and economic clout without neighborhood schools or with beleaguered (often resegregated) public schools that have far more problems and far fewer resources than the for-profit charter schools that skim off their most promising students.[28] Meager tax dollars available in these neighborhoods will go to private managers interested in making a profit rather than building individual and community capacities.

We will see more children socialized into the system of faux meritocracy that characterizes the neoliberal agenda. Children who don't succeed will be blamed for not trying hard enough, and those with all the advantages will be trained to believe that their privilege is earned and therefore deserved. Charter schools like those built on the KIPP model will continue to reinforce their reality that compliance is requisite to success.[29] Reformers will continue to proclaim that their approach will advance civil rights, when in reality, "reform measures in their current frame are resulting in deep and pervasive civil wrongs."[30]

We will see more children being taught by poorly prepared temporary workers who represent cheap, nonunion labor and who have no interest in making a long-term commitment to teaching. The message about teaching is that anyone can do it without special preparation. The message to the already disadvantaged students who have TFA and other alternatively certified personnel in their classrooms is that you don't matter enough to have an experienced, fully licensed, committed professional at the head of the class.[31]

We will see more attacks on teachers' unions, more schemes to incentivize teaching with merit pay approaches, and more efforts to do away with tenure laws and other statutes that protect teachers' right to due process. All of these go hand in hand if your goal is to apply neoliberal policies in schools. If you assume that teachers will not work hard unless there is extra financial gain or they are afraid of being fired, then you need to get rid of unions because they are the way teachers can collectively resist such intrusions on their professional autonomy.[32]

Neoliberal economic policies are based in a kind of social Darwinism. In their survival-of-the-fittest world, it's understood that for a few to win, many will lose. Neoliberal education policies are based on the same logic. The historic function of education as a public good that advances every child's chances in life is being replaced with the neoliberal goal of market-driven schooling that maintains an inherently unequal distribution of wealth while preparing most students for mechanistic, low-paying jobs.[33]

As we speak up about what's best for society, we need to reveal for inspection the consequences of capitulating to the powerful forces behind the neoliberal takeover of schools at the same time we remind others of the value of public schooling in perpetuating our democratic society. Examples of arguments from a variety of sources follow.

Merle McClung has called for "repurposing education" from the business standard of neoliberal reformers to a civic standard based on the original purposes of education proposed by our founding fathers. A lawyer, McClung uses quotes from George Washington, John Adams, Thomas Jefferson, and Benjamin Franklin to show direct ties between education based on a civic standard and the preservation of our constitutional democracy. One example is Franklin's dictum: "We must have a system of public education; its purpose must be to educate our people in their public duties."[34]

McClung argues that the business-model solutions being forced on schools are not a good fit for education problems. He notes that enacting the standards of business models distorts other values, "creating winners and losers, and thus mimicking the top 1% winner-take-all economy that today threatens the very social fabric that ties us together as a nation."[35] The civic standard he proposes would shift the emphasis from competition, profit, and individual success to cooperation, community, and the greater good.

Historians also warn of the dire consequences of forgetting the original purposes of public education in our country. Summarizing the views that characterized eighteenth-century American thinking, Lawrence Cremin wrote, "[R]epublics need an education that would motivate men [and women] to choose public over private interest."[36] Contemporary historian Larry Cuban notes that public schools were created 150 years ago to make sure children "could make reasoned judgments, accept differences of opinions, and fulfill their civic duty to participate in the political and social life of their communities."[37]

Diane Ravitch, historian and education reform critic, reminds us that "[o]ur public education system is a fundamental element of our democratic society. Our public schools have been the pathway to opportunity and a better life for generations." She laments, "At the present time, public education is in peril. Efforts to reform public education are, ironically, diminishing its quality and endangering its very survival."[38]

Teacher education professor Steven Wolk makes a compelling case that schools based on reformers' market-based strategies are actually "schooling for anticitizenship."[39] He calls for giving teachers the time and freedom to prepare children to be well-rounded adults and engaged citizens. Famed educator Deborah Meier warns, "We are witnessing a strategic redefinition of democracy in which the free marketplace of goods and services is not merely a necessary prerequisite, but represented as the highest form of democracy."[40]

The forces pushing for the demise of public education through the application of a business standard are well financed, well organized, and persistently on message. They are successfully using their free-market logic to take over public education. We must resist letting them redefine democracy in neoliberal terms by constantly reminding our potential allies of the negative consequences of market-based approaches to schooling while emphasizing the democratic principles that must be used to repurpose public education in the United States.

DON'T PARTICIPATE IN YOUR OWN DEGRADATION

Returning to the wisdom offered by Erich Fromm: "The fact that millions of people take part in a delusion doesn't make it sane." The deluded view that schools are terrible, teachers are inept, and reformers' tough-minded market-based strategies are the only way to fix things pervades the American consciousness. The propaganda machine behind education reform has fabricated this delusional thinking, and millions of people have bought into it; but that doesn't make it sane. This section is organized as a series of "don'ts" to emphasize ways to avoid falling into the degrading trap that has been set for us.

Don't just expect that this too shall pass. Those of us who have been around for awhile know that dealing with change is a defining characteristic of teaching. The expectation that things will be the same from year to year is not a luxury that teachers have enjoyed since at least the 1980s. Many have adopted the attitude that just riding out the latest educational "innovation" is the best strategy because, like everything in the past, this too shall pass.

Laying low until things change again may have worked for dealing with the educational fads that many states and districts have bought into in the past; but the radical educational reform we are facing now is different. It's different in nature. It's different in scope. And it's different in substance. We can't just wait it out.

The market-based reforms being imposed on public education are not just the latest strategy for teaching reading across the curriculum or the newest school-wide behavior management approach. The reformers' plans are to take over the ways that schools are organized, funded, and run. They want to redefine what schools do and how they do it. They want to reconceptualize what teachers do and how they do it. They want to reconfigure the teaching profession and what it means to be an educator.

The scope of the current reform effort is breathtaking. As was shown in chapter 11, this movement is financed by the wealthiest and promoted by the most powerful individuals in our society. The network of influence behind reform efforts is vast, intricate, and richly funded. Their aims are unabashedly to change the face of education across the nation into a countenance that fits their neoliberal, market-driven ideology.

The sweeping scope of the reform movement requires different strategies than have been needed for making relatively minor changes in the past. Reformers are using targeted legislation, political intimidation, information manipulation, media collusion, and financial coercion to advance their agenda. NCLB, RttT, and the myriad state-level legislative acts that advance the charter movement and take away teacher bargaining rights are prime examples of the ends and means we are up against.

No, these reforms are very different than the pattern of educational innovations that educators have experienced in the past. It would be a grave mistake to think that this movement will pass the way of poorly conceived educational remedies we have ridden out before. Expecting that this too shall pass makes us sitting ducks for those who have targeted teachers and schools for destruction. We need to acknowledge the danger, stand up, and speak out.

Don't start believing the propaganda. The barrage of misinformation about teachers and schooling is so ubiquitous and so consistent it is hard not to be taken in. Teachers are human, we live in the same postmodern world as the rest of society, and we can be fooled into believing that reformers' claims have validity and their proposals have merit. A first step in trying to convince others of fraudulent assertions about the failures of public schools and inadequacies of public school teachers is to be convinced ourselves. A first step in trying to convince others of the dangerous side effects of reformers' remedies is to be convinced ourselves.

The point of debunking the assumptions in Part I of this book is to provide a clear description of what is driving the reform movement and generate a convincing set of arguments for countering it. As a group, teachers are hardworking and committed public servants. They select the profession because they want to shape the future by having a positive impact on young people's lives.[41] For many, it is uncomfortable to challenge what those in positions of authority and power are saying about them and their profession. It's easier to focus on day-to-day classroom interactions than to confront the stark realities of the reform agenda.

By "doing their job" and not reacting to the threats of the reform movement, these teachers may appear to be accepting the assumptions debunked in Part I. With the best of intentions, they may be abetting the cause of those out to undermine their efforts to touch the lives of their students in meaningful ways. In their interactions with administrators, colleagues, parents, and others in the community, their silence may signal tacit agreement with the rationale and acquiescence to the mechanisms of contemporary reform.

When polled regarding the quality of education, teachers and parents almost always rank their own schools higher than they rank schools across the board.[42] This pattern may help explain why some teachers appear to support the aims of the reform movement. It may be that they don't react to the pervasive teacher bashing and school degradation so evident in the reformers' propaganda because they think that *those* teachers and *those* schools are deficient, even though the teachers they know and the schools they work in are fine.

The problems with focusing on the job at hand or thinking that my school is fine (but others need radical restructuring) are clear. Under the proposals of the reform initiatives all around us, teachers' jobs are at risk. What we teach and how we teach are already overly prescribed because of the testing for accountability obsession of the reform movement. Teacher tenure and other due process protections are being stripped away in legislatures and in court challenges supported by reform advocates. Poorly prepared workers are being given alternative licenses so they can replace fully certified, experienced classroom teachers.

Teachers and their partners need to band together to combat the takeover of public schools. If we allow ourselves to be split into "us and them" (those who are fine and those who deserve to be reformed), we are playing into the hands of our enemies. We must present a united front to counter the claims and resist the strategies of those who would remake public education into a for-profit enterprise. The propaganda machine is working overtime; we must work together to be sure voices of reason are heard.

Don't internalize the stigma. It is not uncommon for individuals and groups who are labeled as less than normal by others to self-stigmatize, that is, to internalize the negative stereotypes being projected on them. Self-stigma happens when victims are aware of the stereotypes, agree with them, and apply them to their definitions of self. Self-stigma leads to reduced self-esteem and self-efficacy, so individuals feel bad about who they are and are less likely to believe that they have the capacity to change their circumstances. As a result, those who have internalized the stigma often adopt a "why try" attitude.[43]

Educators are being stereotyped as inadequate, ineffective, inept, and worse by reformers, politicians, the media, and the general public. We are being stigmatized as a problem that needs fixing. It's impossible for anyone reading this book not to be aware of how we are being defined; but we cannot allow ourselves to start believing that our detractors are right, and we must not let others' definitions of our worth impact how we think about ourselves and our profession.

Self-stigmatized individuals often see their futures as inalterable, and they stop trying. We have to gird ourselves and support others to avoid internalizing the stigma being projected on teachers and other educators. We need to refuse the dehumanizing discourse of teacher bashing and do everything in our power to counter it with stories of lived experience, humanity, and caring.[44]

We have to help each other avoid a "why try" attitude at all costs. We can monitor what's going on around us and be aware of the feelings it raises within us without accepting or acting out the labels of those who would demean us and our work. Mostly, we can keep trying and never quit.

Don't quit. Don't quit your job; don't quit the fight. It is easy to understand why teachers are retiring early in frustration or quitting their jobs in protest. The soul is being sucked out of our profession. Our love for teaching and learning, our commitment to shaping the future, our joy in touching the lives of young people are just a blur in the reformers' vision of schooling. It is understandable that experienced teachers would run from conditions that turn their reasons for being there upside down; and it makes sense that new teachers would turn away from mandates that mock their beliefs about what is important in the classroom.

But don't quit. When some of the wisest and most energetic among us leave the field, it advances the strategic objectives of those who want to take over. Reformers prefer a temporary, low-cost, nonunion workforce that will comply without complaint. They are doing everything they can to do away with tenure protections, stop giving raises for education and experience, and set policies that ignore seniority when staffing decisions are made.[45] We are playing into their hands when we quit.

Stay and don't quit the fight. Fight in loud and quiet ways. Speak up at school board meetings and talk with neighbors over coffee. Join in public protests organized by local, state, and national groups and align with coworkers at your school to support each other when things get tough. Lobby government officials to be sure they know the adverse effects of reform policies and be sure to vote for those who support teachers' rights. Take a stand against reforms that hurt children, teachers, and society and look for opportunities to reveal and revel in the inherent joy that meaningful teaching and learning can be.

We become pawns in the education reform game when we participate in our own degradation. Millions of people have bought into the delusional thinking that makes the game appear to be fair; but it is rigged. Our chances of resisting the powerful forces running the game are diminished when we expect that reform is just another educational fad that will go away, start believing the enemy's propaganda, or allow ourselves to internalize the stigma being projected on our profession.

We cannot quit the fight. As Jonathan Kozol wrote in *Letters to a Young Teacher*, "Teachers have to find the will to counteract this madness," because "abject capitulation to unconscionable dictates from incompetent or insecure superiors can be contagious."[46] Teachers must band together to find the will to stay and fight, always looking for big and small openings into which we can inject some sanity.

ENGAGE IN UNION ACTIVITIES THAT PROTECT THE PROFESSION

In France, the words *Liberté, Égalité, Fraternité* are etched into the facades of buildings everywhere. Dating from the French revolution, the national motto of France translates as "freedom, equality, brotherhood." Brotherhood in this case means *community*, as in: We all aspire to liberty and equality, but we cannot achieve them without the assistance of others, without community.[47]

In France, as in many other nations in Europe and around the world, the sentiments of *Fraternité* are lived out in the community of labor unions. It is understood that unions are essential to giving workers a collective say in how they will be treated by private employers and government institutions. Neoliberalism is a global phenomenon, and unions are the targets of wealthy interests and conservative politicians in France, Europe, and beyond. In order to survive, union solidarity and a commitment to *Fraternité* are essential.

So it is with education reformers' goals in the United States. Destroying or rendering ineffectual the labor organizations that have represented teachers is a strategic aim of the reform movement. As was evident in chapter 11, the forces that seek to reshape public education provide substantial financial, political, and ideological support for the attack on teacher unions. Eliminating or silencing unions is a neoliberal dream come true. Protecting and strengthening teacher unions is critical to the survival of public schools.

Building on their successful and heavily publicized effort to hamstring public-sector unions in Wisconsin, education reformers and the wealthy individuals and organizations that back them have launched a concentrated offensive to achieve the same result in other states. Even though Wisconsin has historically been strongly pro-labor and teachers and other union supporters fought hard, the governor and Republican legislators effectively did away with collective bargaining for teachers.

To date, at least five state legislatures have passed laws that mirror the tactics and intent of Wisconsin's union-busting approach. The primary means for destroying teacher unions is to pass legislation that severely limits the issues that can be negotiated in the collective bargaining process. In some cases, teacher unions are not allowed to negotiate anything other than compensation and leave; in others, specific issues like teacher evaluation are prohibited. At the same time, the bills being passed make it much harder for unions to maintain their certifications and collect dues.[48]

It is no surprise that the forces pushing to see teacher unions stripped of any meaningful presence are the same ones promoting radical changes in schooling. It is not by chance that the elements being eliminated from collective bargaining are the ones most closely tied to the reform agenda. Constraining the ability of unions to speak for teachers creates a path of diminished resistance for the implementation of reform initiatives.

This has happened in places like Tennessee, where Kevin Huffman, a Teach for America alumnus, was hired as education commissioner to reform Tennessee public schools. Huffman lead legislative and executive efforts to weaken teacher unions so that education reform could take hold. As a result, collective bargaining rights were stripped, tenure was made meaningless, test scores were mandated to be the most heavily weighted component of teacher evaluation, and a pay scale was implemented that greatly reduced the impact of teachers' education and experience.[49]

Reformers want to apply principles from big business to the operation of schools. Big business has always been about minimizing or eliminating the influence of unions. If teachers are going to resist efforts to destroy our profession by turning education into a giant for-profit enterprise, we have to join together and speak with a united voice. Teacher unions offer our best way to unite and make our collective voices heard.

We need to understand what our opponents know: the pathway to educational reform is much clearer with teacher unions out of the way. We need to engage in union activities that protect the profession. If we have never joined, have let our memberships lapse, or just paid our dues and stood on the sidelines, we need to change. More than ever before, we need to actively support the organizations that represent us at the bargaining table. If we do not, we are clearing the path for radical changes in what we do and how we are treated.

Our engagement needs to be active in the sense that we make sure our union representatives focus on issues that emphasize our desire to be recognized as competent professionals who feel an obligation to do what's right for children and society. Business moguls (of the past and today) do their best to paint organized labor as greedy, self-serving, and bad for the economy. Education reformers play on these perceptions and use them to frame teachers' concerns in the most negative light possible.

The National Education Association[50] and American Federation of Teachers[51] understand what they are up against, and they are working hard to let the general public know that union safeguards for teachers are good for children, families, and society. Front-line teachers and those who support them need to unite around the consistent message that collective bargaining is an essential right—a right that needs to be protected to preserve and improve public schools that meet the needs of all children.

Teacher unions need grassroots support for their efforts to offer alternatives to the radical agenda of the education reform movement. We can acknowledge the need to do a better job of helping struggling teachers get better or move out of the profession; but we can do that without doing away with tenure protections and due process. We can work to improve the quality of education for children in underserved communities; but we can do that without closing neighborhood schools, firing fully licensed teachers, and replacing them with charter schools and temporary labor.

Unions and union members need to do a better job of stressing the value of unionism to society and our economy. Even in parts of the country where conservative politicians have hoodwinked working people into voting against their own economic interests, teachers can show by their actions that union membership means banding together to do what's right for children, families, and communities. They can demonstrate that

> what a good school can be for a student, a good union can be for a mother or father: a path to the middle class, to a productive occupation, and to participation in civic life. [52]

Unions and union members need to emphasize the democratic, social justice dimension that has historically characterized union activity. Without the union movement in this country and around the world, workers would have no counterbalance against those with the most money and power. Their abilities to participate in deciding their own fates would be nil. Without organized labor, we would be living in a plutocracy. Rule by the rich is the antithesis of a democracy,[53] and we need to highlight unions' critical role in combating injustices visited on those who have less by those who have the most.

Teacher unions are under attack. The successes they have achieved in several states will certainly embolden reformers' efforts to emasculate unions in other places. Teachers need to join and engage with unions in order to defend our profession, protect the rights of the children and families we serve, and preserve public schooling in America. Now more than ever, *Fraternité* within our union community and solidarity with those who support our cause are critical.

JOIN WITH OTHERS TO INFLUENCE PUBLIC OPINION AND EDUCATION POLICY MAKING

Don't try to be a lone hero. The image of Don Quixote tilting at windmills is romantic and inspiring; but we need to band with others to resist the gale-force winds of change teachers are facing. Linking with others (inside and outside of professional education) in as many ways as possible builds synergy around our individual commitments and improves our chances of reviving public schooling and protecting the teaching profession.

As individual teachers speak truth to power, our voices are amplified when we join with allies who share our concerns. When parts of the same story are narrated by students, parents, school administrators, and other education professionals, the chances of the story being heard go up dramatically. *Rally together* What follows are selected examples of ways in which some of our allies are telling their story of how radical reformers are threatening public schooling in America.

College students in Wisconsin started Students United for Public Education (SUPE), a "national network of students who are committed to fighting for educational equity in America and to work collectively to organize action that works towards this vision."[54] Within SUPE, committed individuals organized Students Resisting Teach for America, a student-led campaign designed to expose "TFA's role in perpetuating inequality in our schools."[55]

In 2013, members of the Portland Student Union called on fellow high school classmates to boycott the Oregon Assessment of Knowledge and Skills. Student spokesperson Alexia Garcia argued that "the tests take away valuable class time and are ultimately unfair measures of both students and teachers."[56] And the Associated Student Body of Garfield High School gave unanimous support to the teachers in this Seattle school when those teachers successfully resisted giving the Measures of Academic Progress test in 2013.[57]

Ethan Young, a high school student from Knoxville, spoke up at a Knox County Schools Board of Education meeting. Describing the evaluation system imposed on his teachers, Young said,

> These subjective anxiety producers do more damage to teachers' self-esteem than you realize. Erroneous evaluation coupled with strategic compensation presents a punitive model that as a student is like watching your teacher jump through flaming hoops to earn a score. The task of teaching is never quantifiable. If everything I learned in high school is a measurable objective, then I haven't learned anything.[58]

Parents, too, have demonstrated strong support for public education and teachers' resistance to market-based approaches to reform. They have created or helped create organizations and websites that offer support and information to parents opposed to the standardized testing regimes that dominate the reform agenda (e.g., Change the Stakes,[59] Time Out from Testing,[60] and United Opt Out[61]). As an activist parent from upstate New York summarized, "This is our way of civil disobedience."[62]

Juanita Doyon, a parent from Washington State, organized parents to "protect their children from irresponsible, invalid, unproven practice." Her organization, Mothers Against WASL (Washington Assessment of Student Learning), held street corner rallies, produced and distributed anti-testing buttons, wrote letters to the editor, and practiced what Doyon called "grocery line activism" to resist high-stakes testing and other market-driven education policies.[63]

Parents and community activists from across Tennessee formed a group to resist the state's governor and education commissioner's efforts to corporatize Tennessee schools. Called Standing Together for Strong Community Schools (ST4SCS), this group has targeted legislation designed to advance charter schools and vouchers.[64] They also supported a petition calling for the dismissal of the education commissioner and posted a mother's letter to the governor that concluded,

> [Signers of the petition] are FED UP with our schools being "reformed" by those who have no vested interest in Tennessee public education, no children in public school systems, no qualified experience in classrooms, and no business telling teachers and educators how to do their jobs.[65]

Many school superintendents and principals have joined with teachers and parents in resisting the neoliberal incursions of reform advocates. In late 2013, superintendents and school administrators from Suffolk and Nassau counties in New York invited reform critic Diane Ravitch to speak. While they did not commit to a boycott of Common Core tests as Ravitch recommended, these school officials agreed to keep the pressure on the state regarding reforms that drain the public schools.[66]

The Virginia Association of School Superintendents has taken the lead in challenging the use of "standardized tests as the chief 'accountability' metric to evaluate students, teachers, principals and schools for high stakes purposes." At least twenty-eight school boards in Virginia have passed resolutions calling on the state to give schools the freedom to

> promote the joy of teaching and learning with a focus on deep, meaningful, transformative learning, rather than an overemphasis on just covering content that can be easily assessed by standardized tests.[67]

Two principals from Long Island wrote a letter of protest regarding New York State's decision to heavily weight the value-added test scores of students in the annual evaluation of teachers and principals. By late 2012, over one-third of New York principals had signed on to support the document.[68] The same principal group collected over 3,500 signatures in support of an open letter to parents exposing the faulty assumptions and negative outcomes of standardized testing.[69]

Other groups have joined educators and parents in protesting the overuse of standardized tests, notably 120 authors and illustrators of books for children and young people, including Judy Blume, Jane Yolen, and the late Maya Angelou. This group sent a letter to President Obama in which they point out that teachers' and children's love for reading and literature is being crowded out by requirements to evaluate teachers based on high-stakes tests. [70]

Social media, blogs, websites, and other cyber-based communication tools offer teachers and our allies ways to join together to resist the powerful forces behind the reform movement in America. Appendix B includes a list of web-based resources, along with descriptions of the individuals and groups behind them, brief notes on their purposes, and URLs. Several of these resources are cited above, and two representative examples are outlined below.

Diane Ravitch's blog provides updates on anti-reform activities across the nation. It includes links to other blogs and newsfeeds that support teachers and protect public schools. For example, in June 2014, the blog featured the announcement of a protest to be held at the Gates Foundation in Seattle. The post included a list of organizations supporting the protest, notes on speakers at the rally, and an overview of how the Gates Foundation's "experimental reforms have done untold damage to our school system." [71]

The Badass Teachers Association (BATs) is a group of almost fifty thousand teachers, professors, and parents who oppose reformers' efforts to corporatize education. State "affiliates" have emerged in many parts of the country, and BATs' blogspot is a hub of articles, press releases, other blogs, and tweets for those seeking to resist the assault on teachers and public education. For example, in response to the wave of anti-union lawsuits across the country, a 2014 BATs posting exposed the tens of millions of dollars being spent to demonize teacher unions, teachers, and public schools. [72]

Diane Ravitch, the Badass Teachers Association, and all the other individuals and groups interested in fighting off the reform efforts that seem to be outflanking public school advocates understand that a grassroots movement is needed. A successful defense will require the mobilization of the constituencies mentioned in this section and more. Teachers cannot prevail as isolated individuals, and a movement cannot be sustained without multiple, committed stakeholders.

Kevin Kumashiro has written about and lived movement building to resist radical reform efforts in Chicago schools. He reminds us that we cannot hope to change public opinion and education policy if we are talking only to people who already agree with us, and he shares his personal list of what needs to be done to bring about change in educational debates and policies, including meeting with partner organizations, facilitating workshops and public forums for various constituent groups, writing articles and speaking in interviews for the news media, blogging on the Internet, issuing press releases and other public statements, lobbying my elected officials, speaking with my own family and former classmates and neighbors, marching with signs in the street, rallying with bullhorns at the capital, dancing in a flash mob downtown, painting in a public mural in the park, performing with an open mic, and, of course, continuing to do my homework. [73]

For a movement to resist the powerful forces of educational reform to succeed, we need to enlist the support of our allies and follow the example of the individuals and groups featured in this section. Few of us are up to all the to-dos on Kumashiro's list; but there is something on this list that each of us can do, and each of us must do something.

TAKE THE HIGH GROUND, GUARD THE MEANING, REDEFINE HIGH-QUALITY EDUCATION

It sounds redundant to say we should be professional as we seek to reclaim the teaching profession, but our best chance to successfully resist the forces out to get us is to take the high ground and face down the threats with intelligence, persistence, and professionalism. Our strength is in our collective commitment to doing the right thing for America and its children. Expressing our outrage at outrageous things is necessary; putting forth our professional best for the students and communities we serve is imperative.

One way to exercise our professionalism and take the high ground is to offer constructive alternatives to policies that are debilitating our work, damaging children, and destroying public education. Writing in *Education Week*, teacher Justin Minkel advises,

> Teachers need to make sure that when we speak at a school board meeting, approach our superintendent or principal with a new idea, or write a letter to the local paper, we begin with student needs and keep the conversation constructive. That doesn't mean that we hold back from proposing system-shaking changes, but framing potential solutions tends to do more good for our students than reciting familiar problems. [74]

Solution oriented

Another expression of professionalism is to insist on doing what is in the best interests of the children in our care. This has been an integral feature of the acts of resistance featured in this chapter and throughout this book. Educators from Seattle to New York City have aligned with parents and other supporters to take a stand based on the powerful assertion that teachers cannot in good conscience implement policies that hurt students and communities.

In some ways, meaningful learning in schools has become an underground phenomenon, and teachers who care about sparking a lifelong love of learning in their students have had to resort to subverting a system that is obsessed with testing.[75] Teachers guard the meaning when they do right by children, giving them opportunities to enrich their young lives through engaging, transformative, fulfilling experiences with learning.

Better than anyone else, teachers know what high-quality education looks and feels like. We know that the application of business principles works against the purposes and distorts the practices that make public education an invaluable public good. It is up to us to do all we can to improve the educational experiences of every student every day. We must use our professional knowledge, experience, and judgment to demonstrate that we understand what really counts.

Yes, teachers are going through hell, but we must keep going. As we struggle together, we can take hope in the realization that the current state of affairs can get better. We can remember, "contrary to the corporate agenda, that public schools can be places of cooperation, caring, altruism, and concern for the common good."[76] Placing these values in the forefront, we can muster the courage to protect public education and reclaim the profession of teaching. We can't give up or hope others will speak for us. The stakes are too high.

NOTES

1. Downey, M. (2009, July 8). Endangered teachers. *Atlanta Journal-Constitution*, http://www.ajc.com/news/news/opinion/endangered-teachers/nQHhJ/

2. Kohn, A. (2013, September 16). Encouraging educator courage. *Education Week*, http://www.edweek.org/ew/articles/2013/09/18/04kohn.h33.html [pp. 2–3]

3. Gervin, C. W. (2013, November 24). The war on teachers 2: Teachers revolt. *Metro Pulse*, 20–27.

4. Hopson, L. (2013, October 10). Tired teachers: What TN teachers really think about new evaluations. *YouTube*, http://www.youtube.com/watch?v=MRmcBJXEOcA

5. McCoy, L. X. (2013, November 7). Teachers express frustration. *Knoxville News Sentinel*, 1A, 9A.

6. Zeichner, N. (2013). Mapping a teacher boycott in Seattle. *Phi Delta Kappan, 95*(2), 52–58.

7. Roderick, T. (2012). You can't be driven by fear: A portrait of Public School 24. In N. Schniedewind and M. Sapon-Shevin (Eds.), *Educational courage: Resisting the ambush of public education* (pp. 112–119). Boston: Beacon Press.

8. Coleman, S., and Mayorga, E. (2012). "You want me to pay for what?!?": Resisting merit pay and the business model of education. In N. Schniedewind and M. Sapon-Shevin (Eds.), *Educational courage: Resisting the ambush of public education* (pp. 127–135). Boston: Beacon Press.

9. Hogan, K. (2012). The Curie 12: A case for teacher activism. In N. Schniedewind and M. Sapon-Shevin (Eds.), *Educational courage: Resisting the ambush of public education* (pp. 136–141). Boston: Beacon Press. [p. 140]

10. Bruhn, M. (2014). Challenging "Waiting for Superman." *Phi Delta Kappan, 95*(5), 47–51.

11. Hawkins, P. (2014, April 7). My resignation. http://paulinehawkins.com/2014/04/07/my-resignation-letter/ [p. 4]

12. Sluyter, S. (2014, March 23). Resignation letter. *The Washington Post*, http://www.washingtonpost.com/blogs/answer-sheet/wp/2014/03/23/kindergarten-teacher-my-job-is-now-about-tests-and-data-not-children-i-quit/ [p. 6]

13. Maguire, V. (2014, June 10). Is anybody listening to teachers? *Education Week*, http://www.edweek.org/tm/articles/2014/06/10/fp-maguire-speech.html?intc=mvs

14. Gelenian, K. (2013, December 23). The wrong choices on standards. http://susanohanian.org/core.php?id=647

15. Kuhn, J. (2014). *Fear and learning in America: Bad data, good teachers, and the attack on public education.* New York: Teachers College Press.

16. Strauss, V. (2011, February 11). Texas district schools chief issues plea in Alamo-like letter. *Washington Post*, http://voices.washingtonpost.com/answer-sheet/educational-leadership/texas-superintendent-issues-pl.html

17. Kuhn, J. (2011, March 14). John Kuhn reads his Alamo Letter at the Save Texas Schools Rally, *YouTube*, http://www.youtube.com/watch?v=TIMpWVdN-Y4

18. Kuhn. *Fear and learning in America.* [p. 144]

19. Madeloni, B. (2013, February 13). The emotional violence of the accountability regime: Part two. *At the Chalk Face*, http://atthechalkface.com/2013/02/13/the-emotional-violence-of-accountability-part-two/ [p. 5]

20. Whitney, C. (2013, December 26). Teacher: Child abuse in my classroom. *Diane Ravitch's Blog*, http://dianeravitch.net/2013/12/26/teacher-child-abuse-in-my-classroom/ [p. 1]

21. Greene, P. (2014, March 14). Why the hell are we racing anywhere? *Curmudgucation*, http://curmudgucation.blogspot.com/2014/03/why-hell-are-we-racing-anywhere.html

22. Hawkins. My resignation. [pp. 2–3]

23. Hawkins. My resignation; Kohn. Encouraging educator courage.

24. Minkel, J. (2014, April 14). When education policy goes 'clunk': Why teacher-policy-maker partnerships help students. *Education Week*, http://blogs.edweek.org/teachers/teaching_for_triumph/2014/04/when_education_policy_goes_clu.html

25. George, S. (1999). A short history of neo-liberalism. *Global Exchange*, http://www.globalexchange.org/resources/econ101/neoliberalismhist

26. Wolfe, A. (2012, August 19). The ridiculous rise of Ayn Rand. *The Chronicle of Higher Education*, http://chronicle.com/blogs/conversation/2012/08/19/the-ridiculous-rise-of-ayn-rand/

27. George. A short history of neo-liberalism. [pp. 2–3]

28. Madeloni. The emotional violence of the accountability regime.

29. Hartman, A. (2013, February 17). Teach for America's hidden curriculum. *Jacobin Magazine*, https://www.jacobinmag.com/2011/12/teach-for-america/

30. Bryant, J. (2013, February 2). The inconvenient truth of education 'reform.' Campaign for America's Future, http://ourfuture.org/20130202/the-inconvenient-truth-of-education-reform [p. 8]

31. Singhal, N. (2012). Why I quit Teach for America to fight for public education. In N. Schniedewind and M. Sapon-Shevin (Eds.), *Educational courage: Resisting the ambush of public education* (pp. 65–71). Boston: Beacon Press.

32. Hartman. Teach for America's hidden curriculum.

33. Schniedewind, N. (2012). A short history of the ambush of public education. In N. Schniedewind and M. Sapon-Shevin (Eds.), *Educational courage: Resisting the ambush of public education* (pp. 4–22). Boston: Beacon Press.

34. McClung, M. (2013). Repurposing education. *Phi Delta Kappan, 94*(8), 37–39. [p. 38]

35. McClung. Repurposing education. [p. 39]

36. Cremin, L. A. (1980). *American education: The national experience, 1783–1896.* New York: Harper and Row. [p. 2]

37. Cuban, L. (2001, November 7). Why bad reforms won't give us good schools. *American Prospect*, http://prospect.org/article/why-bad-reforms-wont-give-us-good-schools [p. 3]

38. Ravitch, D. (2010). *The death and life of the great American school system: How testing and choice are undermining education.* New York: Perseus Books. [pp. 241–242]

39. Wolk, S. (2007). Why go to school? *Phi Delta Kappan, 88*(9), 648–658. [p. 651]

40. Meier, D. (2012). Forward. In M. Fabricant and M. Fine, *Charter schools and the corporate makeover of public education: What's at stake?* New York: Teachers College Press. [p. ix]

41. Phillips, M. B., and Hatch, J. A. (2000). Why teach? Prospective teachers' reasons for entering the profession. *Journal of Early Childhood Teacher Education, 21,* 373–384

42. Gallup (2014, June 20). Education: Gallup historical trends. *Gallup Website,* http://www.gallup.com/poll/1612/education.aspx

43. Corrigan, P. W., Larson, J. E., and Rusch, N. (2009). Self-stigma and the "why try" effect: Impact on life goals and evidence-based practices. *World Psychiatry, 8*(2), 75–81.

44. Madeloni. The emotional violence of the accountability regime.

45. TNTP. (July 15, 2014). *Shortchanged: The hidden cost of lockstep teacher pay.* TNTP, http://tntp.org/publications/view/retention-and-school-culture/shortchanged-the-hidden-costs-of-lockstep-teacher-pay

46. Kozol, J. (2007). *Letters to a young teacher.* New York: Random House. [pp. 129–130]

47. Nora, P. (1996). *Realms of memory: The construction of the French past.* New York: Columbia University Press.

48. Rosenthal, D. M. (2014). What education reformers should do about collective bargaining. *Phi Delta Kappan, 95*(5), 58–62.

49. Gervin. The war on teachers 2.

50. National Education Association. (2008, July). NEA policy paper: Great public schools for every student by 2020. NEA, http://www.nea.org/home/18214.htm

51. American Federation of Teachers. (2012, July). The American Federation of Teachers' quality education agenda. AFT, http://www.aft.org/newspubs/press/qualityagenda.cfm

52. Rosenthal. What education reformers should do about collective bargaining. [p. 60]

53. Moyers, B. (2010, April 30). *Bill Moyer's journal.* Public Broadcasting System, http://www.pbs.org/moyers/journal/04302010/transcript2.html

54. Students United for Public Education website, http://supe.k12newsnetwork.com/

55. Students Resisting Teach for America website, http://studentsresistingtfa.k12newsnetwork.com/

56. Dungca, N. (2013, February 1). Portland Public Schools students push standardized test boycott. *The Oregonian,* http://www.oregonlive.com/portland/index.ssf/2013/02/portland_public_schools_studen_1.html [p. 1]

57. Zeichner. Mapping a teacher boycott in Seattle.

58. McCoy. Teachers express frustration. [p. 1A]

59. Change the Stakes website, http://changethestakes.wordpress.com/

60. Time Out from Testing website, http://timeoutfromtesting.org/

61. United Opt Out website, http://unitedoptout.com/

62. Altman, A. (2014, April 21). Skipping out: Common Core tests spark a parent revolt. *Time,* 12.

63. Doyon, J. (2012). We are not the backlash: We are the resistance. In N. Schniedewind and M. Sapon-Shevin (Eds.), *Educational courage: Resisting the ambush of public education* (pp. 148–154). Boston: Beacon Press. [p. 154]

64. Standing Together for Strong Community Schools website, http://strongcommunityschools.wordpress.com/

65. Mnpsparent. (2013, June 27). Momma Bear and West TN moms stand up to Haslam. Standing Together for Strong Community Schools Website, http://strongcommunityschools.wordpress.com/2013/06/27/momma-bear-stand-up-to-haslam/

66. Tyrrell, J. (2013, November 19). Diane Ravitch calls for Common Core boycott, refusal to give tests. *Newsday,* http://www.newsday.com/long-island/education/diane-ravitch-calls-for-common-core-boycott-refusal-to-give-tests-1.6465462

67. Strauss, V. (2013, October 27). Virginia schools boards pass anti-SOL resolutions. *The Washington Post,* http://www.washingtonpost.com/blogs/answer-sheet/wp/2013/10/27/virginia-schools-boards-pass-anti-sol-resolutions/ [pp. 1, 3]

68. New York Principals (2013). APPR paper. New York Principals website, http://www.newyorkprincipals.org/appr-paper

69. New York Principals. (2014). Letter to parents about testing. New York Principals website, http://www.newyorkprincipals.org/letter-to-parents-about-testing

70. Strauss, V. (2013, October 22). Top authors—including Maya Angelou—urge Obama to curb standardized testing. *The Washington Post*, http://www.washingtonpost.com/blogs/answer-sheet/wp/2013/10/22/top-authors-including-maya-angelou-urge-obama-to-curb-standardized-testing/

71. Ravitch, D. (2014, June 25). Protest to be held tomorrow at Gates Foundation in Seattle. *Diane Ravitch Blog*, http://dianeravitch.net/2014/06/25/protest-to-be-held-tomorrow-at-gates-foundation-in-seattle/

72. Naison, M. (2014, June 25). The staggering amounts of money spent to show teachers and teachers unions are to blame for inequality. *Badass Teachers Association*, http://badassteachers.blogspot.com/

73. Kumashiro, K. K. (2012). *Bad teacher: How blaming teachers distorts the bigger picture.* New York: Teachers College Press. [p. 87]

74. Minkel, J. (2014, April 14). When education policy goes 'clunk': Why teacher-policy-maker partnerships help students. *Education Week*, http://blogs.edweek.org/teachers/teaching_for_triumph/2014/04/when_education_policy_goes_clu.html [p. 2]

75. Hatch, J. A. (2007). Learning as a subversive activity. *Phi Delta Kappan, 89*, 310–311.

76. Schniedewind, N, and Sapon-Shevin, M. (2012). Postscript. In N. Schniedewind and M. Sapon-Shevin (Eds.), *Educational courage: Resisting the ambush of public education* (pp. 112–119). Boston: Beacon Press. [p. 204]

Appendix A: ALEC Model Legislation Examples

CAREER LADDER OPPORTUNITY ACT (1995)*

http://www.alec.org/model-legislation/career-ladder-opportunity-act/**

Summary: The Career Ladder Opportunity Act requires school districts to adopt extraordinary performance pay plans for elementary and secondary public school teachers who demonstrate success in the classroom. The local school district must design the plan in consultation with teachers and administrators. Since reward systems in the past have often failed because of premature abandonment, the district must keep the plan for three years and make improvements on it when necessary.

TEACHER QUALITY AND RECOGNITION DEMONSTRATION ACT (2002)

http://www.alec.org/model-legislation/teacher-quality-and-recognition-demonstration-act/

Summary: This bill is directed toward creating a new structure of the current teaching system that will promote the retention and reward of good teachers and attract new talent to the profession. This bill establishes Teacher Quality Demonstration projects wherein local education agencies are exempt from education rules and regulations regarding teacher certification, tenure, recruitment, and compensation, and are granted funding for the purpose of creating new models of teacher hiring, professional growth and development, compensation, and recruitment.

TEACHER CHOICE COMPENSATION ACT (2002)

http://www.alec.org/model-legislation/teacher-choice-compensation-act/

Summary: This act creates a program whereby teachers may be eligible for performance-based salary stipends if they opt out of their permanent contract and meet measurable student performance goals based on a value-added test instrument developed by the state department of education.

VIRTUAL PUBLIC SCHOOLS ACT (2005)

http://www.alec.org/model-legislation/the-virtual-public-schools-act/

Summary: Providing a broader range of educational options to parents and utilizing existing resources, along with technology, may help students improve their academic achievement. Virtual schools established in this article provide families with an alternative choice to access additional educational resources. Nothing in this bill shall preclude the use of computer- and Internet-based instruction for students in a virtual or remote setting.

ALTERNATIVE CERTIFICATION ACT (2006)

http://www.alec.org/model-legislation/alternative-certification-act/

Summary: Certification requirements that correspond to state-approved education programs in most states prevent many individuals from entering the teaching profession. To obtain an education degree, students must often complete requirements in educational methods, theory, and style rather than in-depth study in a chosen subject area. Comprehensive alternative certification programs improve teacher quality by opening up the profession to well-educated, qualified, and mature individuals. States should enact alternative teacher certification programs to prepare persons with subject area expertise and life experience to become teachers through a demonstration of competency and a comprehensive mentoring program.

THE NEXT GENERATION CHARTER SCHOOLS ACT (2007)

http://www.alec.org/?post_type=model-legislation&s=next+generation+charter+schools+act

Summary: Charter schools serve a distinct purpose in supporting innovations and best practices that can be adopted among all public schools. There must be a variety of public institutions that can authorize the establishment of charter schools as defined by law. Therefore, the purpose of this act is to establish that existing (or new) public entities may be created to approve and monitor charter schools in addition to public school district boards. This act also removes procedural and funding barriers to charter school success.

FAMILY EDUCATION SAVINGS ACCOUNT ACT (2008)

http://www.alec.org/model-legislation/the-family-education-savings-account-act/

Summary: The Family Education Savings Account Act would create a tax deduction/credit for contributions made by state taxpayers into students' Coverdell education savings accounts, which allow tax-free savings for both K-12 and higher education expenses.

GREAT SCHOOLS TAX CREDIT (2009)

http://www.alec.org/model-legislation/the-great-schools-tax-credit-program-act-scholarship-tax-credits/

Summary: The Great Schools Tax Credit Program authorizes a tax credit for individual and corporate contributions to organizations that provide educational scholarships to eligible students so they can attend qualifying public or private schools of their parents' choice.

PARENTAL CHOICE SCHOLARSHIP PROGRAM ACT (2009)

http://www.alec.org/model-legislation/the-parental-choice-scholarship-program-act-universal-eligibility/

Summary: The Parental Choice Scholarship Program Act creates a scholarship program that provides all children the option to attend the public or private elementary or secondary school of their parents' choice.

INNOVATION SCHOOLS AND SCHOOL DISTRICTS ACT (2009)

http://www.alec.org/model-legislation/the-innovation-schools-and-school-districts-act/

Summary: The Innovation Schools and School Districts Act creates a mechanism for schools, groups of schools, and districts to adopt plans that try new ways of delivering instruction and/or allocating resources. It creates a new classification of school districts, "Districts of Innovation," that have one or more schools implementing these plans. Districts of innovation are provided a greater degree of autonomy and can waive some statutory requirements.

ONLINE LEARNING CLEARINGHOUSE ACT (2010)

http://www.alec.org/model-legislation/online-learning-clearinghouse-act/

Summary: The Online Learning Clearinghouse Act creates a clearinghouse through which school districts may offer their computer-based courses to students of other school districts.

GREAT TEACHERS AND LEADERS ACT (2010)

http://www.alec.org/model-legislation/great-teachers-and-leaders-act/

Summary: The Great Teachers and Leaders Act reforms the practice of tenure, known as nonprobationary status in some states. Teachers can earn tenure after three years of sufficient student academic growth; tenure is revocable following two consecutive years of insufficient growth. The Council for Educator Effectiveness will define teacher effectiveness and come up with parameters for an evaluation system that requires 50 percent of a teacher's evaluation to be based on student achievement using multiple measures. The act requires principals to be evaluated annually, with 50 percent of the evaluation based on student achievement and their ability to develop teachers in their buildings and increase their effectiveness. The act eliminates the practice of forced teacher placement (slotting teachers in schools without their or the principal's consent) and replaces it with mutual consent hiring using the Chicago model (principals and teachers must agree to teacher placements and teachers who are not selected serve as substitutes for a year and, if not selected in the subsequent hiring cycle, are put on unpaid leave). The act allows school districts to make reduction-in-force decisions based on teacher performance rather than on seniority.

OPEN ENROLLMENT ACT (2011)

http://www.alec.org/model-legislation/the-open-enrollment-act/

Summary: The Open Enrollment Act stipulates that a student may attend any public school or program in the state. The legislation allows the parents of the student to apply for attendance in any nonresident school, either within or outside the district of residence. The nonresident school would advise the parent within a reasonable time if the application was accepted. No school district can be obligated to change existing school structures or program guidelines. No school can reject an application except for lack of space, existing eligibility criteria, desegregation plan requirements, expulsion record, or late enrollment.

CHARTER SCHOOL GROWTH AND QUALITY ACT (2011)

http://www.alec.org/model-legislation/charter-school-growth-with-quality-act/

Summary: The Charter School Growth with Quality Act would expand quality public education opportunities for all children by establishing a state public charter school commission to serve as an independent statewide charter authorizer.

* Sample bills are listed in chronological order to show evolvement of ALEC policy approaches.
** Links go directly to ALEC's website.

Appendix B: Organizations, Websites, and Blogs

Name: Alfie Kohn http://www.alfiekohn.org/index.php
Who: This is the author website for Alfie Kohn.
Purpose: Kohn has been described as "perhaps the country's most outspoken critic of education's fixation on grades [and] test scores."

Name: The Answer Sheet http://www.washingtonpost.com/blogs/answer-sheet/
Who: This is a blog by Valerie Strauss for the *Washington Post*.
Purpose: "Valerie Strauss writes about everything that matters in education."

Name: At the Chalk Face http://atthechalkface.com/
Who: At the Chalk Face is a blog written by "educated educators talking education." These educators also discuss education on their weekly radio show entitled, *Chalk Face Radio*.
Purpose: This blog endeavors "to establish an alternative space to discuss education reform from an entirely progressive perspective."

Name: Badass Teachers Association (BATs) http://badassteachers.blogspot.com/
Who: BATs started as an idea by Mark Naison, and was co-founded by him and Priscilla Sanstead. BATs has grown to include a group of professors, teachers, and parents against corporate education.
Purpose: This organization "is for every teacher who refuses to be blamed for the failure of our society to erase poverty and inequality, and

refuses to accept assessments, tests and evaluations imposed by those who have contempt for real teaching and learning."

Name: Bridging Differences http://blogs.edweek.org/edweek/Bridging-Differences/
Who: This is a blog written by noted educator Deborah Meier for *Education Week*.
Purpose: Deborah Meier "blogs with different education thinkers on the big issues affecting students, teachers, and schools."

Name: Broader, Bolder Approach to Education http://www.boldapproach.org/
Who: "The BBA was convened in 2008 by Economic Policy Institute President Larry Mishel." Elaine Weiss is the national coordinator.
Purpose: "The Broader Bolder Approach to Education is a national campaign that acknowledges the impact of social and economic disadvantage on schools and students and proposes evidence-based policies to improve schools and remedy conditions that limit many children's readiness to learn."

Name: Campaign for America's Future http://ourfuture.org/
Who: This is a blog lead by codirectors Robert Borosage and Roger Hickey.
Purpose: The campaign advances a progressive economic agenda and a vision of the future that works for all, not simply the few. Bloggers defend public education from its attackers and show the way toward accessible education for all.

Name: Center for Media and Democracy's PR Watch http://www.prwatch.org
Who: Lisa Graves is the executive director/editor-in-chief of this national, nonprofit organization.
Purpose: "CMD's niche is investigating and exposing the undue influence of corporations and front groups on public policy."

Name: Change the Stakes http://changethestakes.wordpress.com/
Who: Change the Stakes is a website run by a group of parents and educators concerned with the harm high-stakes testing is doing to children and schools.
Purpose: Change the Stakes aims to join hands with parents and community members "to improve teaching and learning opportunities for all children."

Name: Charter School Scandals http://charterschoolscandals.blogspot.com/
Who: This blog is written by Sharon Higgins.
Purpose: Charter School Scandals is "a compilation of news articles about charter schools' . . . questionable, unethical, borderline-legal, or illegal activities."

Name: Class Size Matters http://www.classsizematters.org/
Who: Class Size Matters is an organization founded and directed by Leonie Haimson.
Purpose: It is a nonprofit organization that advocates for smaller classes in NYC's public schools and the nation as a whole.

Name: Curmudgucation http://curmudgucation.blogspot.com/
Who: This is a blog written by Peter Greene, a retired teacher.
Purpose: Greene's aim is to stand up for public education and educators.

Name: Deutsch29 http://deutsch29.wordpress.com/
Who: This blog is by Louisiana public school teacher Mercedes Schneider.
Purpose: It focuses on local and national education issues with topics such as vouchers, TFA, ALEC, charter schools, high-stakes testing, and public school funding.

Name: Diane Ravitch http://dianeravitch.net/
Who: This is the blog of leading reform critic Diane Ravitch.
Purpose: Ravitch calls it "a site to discuss better education for all."

Name: Ed Notes Online http://ednotesonline.blogspot.com/
Who: This blog is written by Norm Scott, retired teacher of thirty years.
Purpose: Ed Notes provides information on "current ed issues, organizing activities around fighting for public education in NYC and beyond and exposing the motives behind the education deformers."

Name: Educationalchemy http://educationalchemy.com/
Who: Those who run this blog are not identified.
Purpose: This is a blog dedicated to "democracy, public education, and the power of the imagination to fight corporate greed."

Name: Education Talk New Orleans http://edutalknola.com/
Who: Education Talk New Orleans is written by Karran Harper Royal, a public school parent.

Purpose: "This blog is intended to give the reader a different perspective on education reforms in New Orleans and across the country."

Name: EduSanity http://www.edusanity.com/
Who: EduSanity is coauthored by Jason Endacott and Christian Goering.
Purpose: The blog represents "a concerted effort to restore rational, grounded perspectives to the discourse about K-16 education in America."

Name: Edushyster http://edushyster.com/
Who: Jennifer Berkshire authors this blog.
Purpose: Berkshire's purpose is to keep an eye on the "corporate education agenda."

Name: FairTest http://fairtest.org/
Who: FairTest is an organization affiliated with the National Center for Fair and Open Testing.
Purpose: FairTest "works to end the misuses and flaws of standardized testing and to ensure that evaluation of students, teachers and schools is fair, open, valid and educationally beneficial."

Name: Grassroots Education Movement (GEM) http://gemnyc.org/
Who: GEM is a coalition of activist groups in New York City.
Purpose: "The Grassroots Education Movement educates, organizes, and mobilizes educators, parents, students and communities to defend public education."

Name: Great Schools for America http://greatschoolsforamerica.org/
Who: Great Schools for America is an organization started by educator Debby Mayer.
Purpose: The organization's purpose is to "advocate for quality public schools, free from corporate control."

Name: Institute for Democratic Education in America (IDEA) http://democraticeducation.org/index.php/blog/
Who: IDEA is an organization started by Dana Bennis and Melia Dicker.
Purpose: IDEA is a national effort to connect education with our nation's democratic values and "grow the capacity of the people to reclaim the 'public' in public education."

Name: Living in Dialogue http://blogs.edweek.org/teachers/living-in-dialogue/
Who: This blog is written by veteran teacher Anthony Cody for *Education Week*.

Purpose: Cody's purpose is to create " a dialogue on education reform and teaching for change and deep learning."

Name: National Education Policy Center (NEPC) http://nepc.colorado. edu/
Who: The director of NEPC is Kevin G. Welner.
Purpose: NEPC's goal is to "produce and disseminate high-quality, peer-reviewed research to inform education policy discussions."

Name: Network for Public Education http://www.network forpubliceducation.org/
Who: The Network for Public Education was cofounded by Anthony Cody. The current president is Diane Ravitch.
Purpose: "The Network for Public Education is an advocacy group whose goal is to fight to protect, preserve and strengthen our public school system, an essential institution in a democratic society."

Name: New Jersey Teacher Activist Group (NJTAG) http://www.njtag. org/
Who: NJTAG is a grassroots democratic group of New Jersey educators united in efforts to both save and transform public education.
Purpose: "The Mission of the New Jersey Teacher Activist Group (NJTAG) is to ensure equitable access to quality, public, progressive educational opportunities for ALL children and to foster and support teacher agency and activism both inside and outside the classroom."

Name: Parents United for Responsible Education (PURE) http:// pureparents.org/
Who: PURE was started by a group of Chicago parents and teachers.
Purpose: "PURE exists to support and assure a high quality public education for all children by informing parents about education issues and parents' rights, bringing parents into the decision making process, empowering parents in their role as advocates for their children, and assisting them in their interactions within the school system."

Name: Public School Shakedown http://www.publicschoolshakedown. org/
Who: *Progressive Magazine* launched the Public School Shakedown website.
Purpose: Public School Shakedown seeks to "show what is at stake as the right wing begins to dismantle public education, follow the money, expose the privatizers, and help parents, teachers, and concerned citizens understand what is going on and connect with each other to stick up for schools."

Name: Reconsidering TFA http://reconsideringtfa.wordpress.com/
Who: This blog is written by education activist Demian Godon.
Purpose: "Reconsidering TFA was launched to provide a critical perspective on an organization that is attracting significant attention in education reform discussions."

Name: Red4EdNC http://red4ednc.com/
Who: This is a blog by North Carolina teachers.
Purpose: Red4EdNC seeks to "inform North Carolinians of the challenges facing public education and demonstrate their support of public schools by wearing red on Wednesdays."

Name: Rethinking Schools http://www.rethinkingschools.org/index. shtml
Who: Rethinking Schools is a nonprofit organization started by Milwaukee-area teachers, which has become an international organization.
Purpose: "Rethinking Schools is a nonprofit publisher and advocacy organization dedicated to sustaining and strengthening public education through social justice teaching and education activism."

Name: Save Our Schools http://saveourschoolsmarch.org/
Who: This is an organization made up of educators, parents, students, and concerned citizens.
Purpose: "Save Our Schools is dedicated to public education as the cornerstone of a democratic society. We are committed to education policy and actions that allow students, teachers, families, and communities to work together to meet the needs of all children."

Name: Standing Together for Strong Community Schools (ST4SCS) http://strongcommunityschools.wordpress.com/
Who: This is an advocacy group of parents and community activists from across Tennessee.
Purpose: ST4SCS aims to "educate legislators, parents, and citizens across the state about the dire consequences of legislation, pushed by special interest groups, that will negatively impact our public schools, teachers and tax dollars."

Name: Students Resisting TFA http://studentsresistingtfa. k12newsnetwork.com/
Who: Students Resisting TFA is a website hosted by Students United for Public Education.

Purpose: This campaign was created to build a resistance movement to the model and approach of Teach for America (TFA).

Name: Students United for Public Education (SUPE) http://supe.k12newsnetwork.com/
Who: SUPE is a community-based organization started by college students in Wisconsin.
Purpose: SUPE works with community members to "defend public education from its attackers."

Name: Susan Ohanian http://www.susanohanian.org/index.php
Who: This is the website of reform critic Susan Ohanian.
Purpose: Ohanian's website is "a treasure trove of information and work against the Educational-Industrial Complex so-called reforms."

Name: Teachers of Conscience http://teachersofconscience.wordpress.com/
Who: "This blog was created by a group of public school teachers in New York City concerned about market-based reforms and the future of public education."
Purpose: Teachers of Conscience is "fighting to preserve the dignity of the teaching profession from the damage done by market-based reform."

Name: Teachers Talk Testing http://www.teacherstalktesting.com/
Who: "Teachers Talk Testing grew out of the PS 321 Testing Task Force. The Testing Task Force is a group of parents and teachers coming together to extend community-wide dialogue on the impacts of federal, state, and NYC Department of Ed policies in the daily life of our children and teachers."
Purpose: The purpose of this blog is to "advocate for the fair and valid use of tests in a thoughtful manner that truly measures student learning and growth."

Name: Time Out from Testing http://timeoutfromtesting.org/
Who: "Time Out From Testing is a statewide coalition of parent, educator, business, community, and civil rights organizations in New York State committed to a 'time-out' from excessive and high stakes exams."
Purpose: "We call for a comprehensive review of the Regents exams and state-initiated 4th and 8th grade standardized tests and the impact they have had on our children, our schools, and our communities."

Name: United Opt Out http://unitedoptout.com/
Who: United Opt Out is a nonprofit organization incorporated in Florida. "Members of this site are parents, educators, students and social activists

who are dedicated to the elimination of high stakes testing in public education."

Purpose: "We use this site to collaborate, exchange ideas, support one another, share information and initiate collective local and national actions to end the reign of fear and terror promoted by the high stakes testing agenda."

Index